Constructing Europe

25 Years of Architecture

European Union Prize
for Contemporary Architecture
Mies van der Rohe Award

Prefaces

1988 – 2013 Photographic Survey

Timeline

José Manuel Barroso
President of the European Commission

Since the very beginning, Europe has been a continent of culture and creativity. Our music, literature, visual arts and architecture bind us together much beyond markets, fostering mutual understanding and a sense of shared values. They also help us imagine a common future.

Investment in the cultural and creative sectors is not just a necessity for us as individuals but also for our societies and economies. These sectors have an enormous potential to promote smart, sustainable and inclusive growth, by creating jobs, stimulating innovation and helping build more cohesive societies.

The European Commission has supported them in many ways, notably through the Culture and MEDIA programmes, which we propose to integrate as of 2014 in a new framework programme appropriately called Creative Europe. The future programme will continue to support artists and cultural professionals in developing their skills and working across borders; it will provide easier access to funding and help increase Europe's competitiveness in the culture and audio-visual sectors.

Establishing prizes to projects or people who show excellence in the field of cultural heritage, in pop music, in contemporary literature or in architecture is one way of valorising the excellence of the European creative and cultural sectors. The European Union Prize for Contemporary Architecture - Mies van der Rohe Award was created twenty-five years ago because we believed that there is an enormous talent in Europe in the architecture sector – and the history of the Prize has proven us right in an outstanding manner.

The winners, among the best architects in the world, are European architects, working in Europe for European clients, but they are also of international calibre and work on a global scale. The emerging architects who have received special mentions have brought fresh ideas and energy into the Prize landscape. Over time, the prize has drawn the attention of potential public and private clients, of the media, and ultimately of the general public, to the value of architecture for all of us. This positive message about European architecture is all the more needed in the current challenging times.

I have had the chance to visit some of the winning works and I was touched by their vision and by the innovative solutions they can bring to problems of our times – on a technological, environmental and social level. These outstanding architectural works significantly contribute to the creation of the sustainable European city of tomorrow, by promoting better harmony between human beings and their environment.

"Architecture is the will of an epoch translated into space," said Ludwig Mies van der Rohe, one of the most famous architects of the last century. I believe the European Union Prize for Contemporary Architecture – which is aptly named after him – is a vivid example of the will of our times to integrate individuals, communities and their environments into the diversity of local traditions, which Europe is so rich of. At the same time, this celebration of excellence and diversity is also what gives to the Prize a distinct European flavour.

I would like to take this opportunity to thank the Fundació Mies van der Rohe for their profound dedication and expertise put at the service of European architecture. Last, I wish all the architects, whose works are presented in this book a successful international career, inspiring future generations.

Xavier Trias
Mayor of Barcelona

Together with the European Commission, since 1988 the Fundació Mies van der Rohe has been responsible for organising the European Union Prize for Contemporary Architecture - Mies van der Rohe Award.

This event reinforces the concept of Barcelona as a city committed to contemporary urban development based on quality architecture. A city that fosters intelligent urban planning that prioritises people and is focussed on the configuration of human-scale productive districts and the application of energy efficiency and environmental quality strategies. The Prize, whose purpose is to acknowledge architectural quality throughout Europe, also serves to place Barcelona internationally at the vanguard of architecture.

All the editions of the Prize have so far highlighted the creative potential and innovative capacity of today's European architects. The organisation of each award edition is carried out through the collaboration of the independent experts, the national architects associations, the Advisory Committee and a jury of renowned professionals: acclaimed architects and critics who have contributed to the attainment of major international recognition.

This Prize constitutes a compilation of European architects' recent output through a wide selection of outstanding works of all kinds, which together provide a panoramic view of contemporary European architecture. Thanks to its contribution to the positive development of cities and to the propagation of contemporary architecture, the Prize makes it possible for the task to continue.

Barcelona, as promoter of and host to the Prize, has become consolidated on the European level as a benchmark in terms of the best values of contemporary architecture, fruit of its endeavours to improve the quality of life of the people who live and work in the city.

Celebrating the 25th anniversary of the Prize is an opportunity both to highlight the successes we have achieved and to reflect on the future of these awards. This new period opens at a time when the whole of Europe is facing a difficult situation, which invites us to think about setting new goals to continue fostering the development of good European architecture.

Spirit

Giovanna Carnevali
Director, Fundació
Mies van der Rohe

*'The new times are here with us; they exist regardless of whether we want them or not. [...]
The only decisive thing is how to assert ourselves in these given circumstances.'* [1]
Mies van der Rohe

History tells us that in medieval Germany the twenty-fifth anniversary of a married couple was celebrated as recognition of their having managed to maintain a harmonious relationship over a long period of time.

Commemorating the 25th anniversary of the European Union Prize for Contemporary Architecture - Mies van der Rohe Award is tantamount to celebrating the achievement of having reached the present day with our enthusiasm for fostering innovation and quality in architecture entirely intact. On the other hand, however, it also calls for an exercise in retrospective meditation and a necessary reflection that will enable us to continue for a further twenty-five years rewarding architecture's ability to understand the circumstances of the moment and exploit them at the service of a society in constant evolution.

Mies' declaration concerning *'the new times',* their inexorable existence and the potential we carry inside to face and evaluate the possibilities that each moment offers is particularly opportune in the current situation.

Mies wrote this at a time when Europe was immersed in an economic and political crisis that broke out at the end of the 1920s, the natural consequence of which was a dearth of professional opportunities, which the architect took advantage of to conduct a research project whose result would be a benchmark by which to understand the development of architecture during all the periods that came after him.

Eighty years later, in the midst of what in some ways is a similar situation, it would be expedient to change the word 'crisis' for 'point of inflexion', in allusion to the opportunity to engage in serene reflection on the needs of a society aware of the fact that a system is nearing exhaustion.

My appointment as Director of the Fundació Mies van der Rohe has coincided with this point of inflexion and, consequently, it is my intention to contribute to converting this period into an opportunity to listen to a society that demands accountability for the present and future of the world in which we live.

When speaking about the Fundació and the Prize, I must of necessity refer to their origin: the Pavilion that the architect designed and built for the 1929 Barcelona World Exhibition.

1. Closing address at the Vth *Deutscher Werkbund* congress held in Vienna in June 1930.

The decision taken, years later, to reconstruct this architectural landmark is evidence of the significance of a work whose preservation was regarded as essential by virtue of its exceptional nature. True to this same spirit, the Award was instituted with the will to acknowledge not only innovation in the material and technical realms but also excellence in all the facets that together constitute a work of architecture.

New technologies have come to foster acceleration of activity in all fields, thereby generating expectations of constant innovation. Architecture, which represents a culture, must not miss the opportunity to project itself towards the future by exploiting the cultural, technological and economic circumstances of its own period. Nonetheless, as I commented earlier, perhaps the moment has come to stop and listen to the demands of society in these times of change, to engage in an exercise of inner searching in order to analyse the results of the evolution of architecture in recent years and to establish new objectives. It seems that the need has arisen to ask whether a unanimous view exists or whether we must pool the different points of view to establish the aspects to be valued of a specific work.

While to maintain its balance history might require shock therapies capable of transforming a culture and of placing within reach of society those technical and technological advances through an aesthetic evolution able to represent the 'spirit of the times', it is equally true that not only technology leads to progress: social development itself, in a kind of vicious circle, nurtures the cultural changes it generates. Nevertheless, these changes materialise in a time gap between innovation and interiorisation. And it is this fact that provides us with the opportunity to constantly and meticulously observe what society, of which we form part, calls for to satisfy its physical, intellectual and spiritual needs.

'Everything I read was about what influences architecture. When I read sociology, I wanted to know which ideas might really be influential in our times. I didn't want to change time, I wanted to express time; that was my entire project.' [2]
Mies van der Rohe

In recent years the evolution of telecommunications, the genesis of a digital universe and the so-called collective brain have placed multidisciplinary knowledge within our reach that, in the past, architects like Mies sought in books, thereby revealing through their efforts the need to acquire the kind of knowledge that would allow them to raise questions such as the nature of the essence of architecture.

2. Mies van der Rohe in conversation with Peter Blake, in *Conversaciones con Mies van der Rohe*. Ed. Gustavo Gili, Barcelona, 2006.

With this question, the answer to which is ineffable, and far from proposing merely theoretical exercises nurtured by a parallel discourse, Mies exhibited his intellectual efforts in the form of the architectural object, which as such he based on a set of prior conditioning factors among which the site played an especially significant role together with the suitable use of technology and technics and the discerning choice of materials. In this way, he anticipated the needs of a society that would soon demand a new way of being in the world.

At the present time, the proliferation of interconnected information units requires us, first of all, to ask ourselves what our objectives are and how we may obtain the tools we need to meet them. Because an initial step consists of selecting the information necessary to respond to the socio-cultural expectations of the moment and to learn to navigate in search of that knowledge that will help us come increasingly closer to an understanding of the aim of our task. Decisive keys in the development of the digital universe are opinion communities, blogs, forums and social networks, which provide us with a unique opportunity to establish a relationship with the potential and ultimately compulsory users of architecture, in an act of heeding an instrument that contributes to fostering genuine democracy.

Many complementary forms of knowledge have gradually placed us in greater proximity to the user over the space of over a century. Since the 1800s, the theory of perception has been in constant evolution and has placed within our reach the possibility of understanding what the mechanisms are through which the environment influences our state of mind and, by extension, all aspects of our lives. Technology has revolutionised the way we conceive, generate and experience space. The relations between people and objects are increasingly mediatised. The development of environmental studies has made people aware of the importance of regulating consumption of specific energy resources, etc.

Architects have echoed all this knowledge by seeking the way to implement it in innovative projects, thereby revealing their ability to react and adapt to change and their sensitivity towards and commitment to ongoing training.

We should ask ourselves, however, whether the pace marked by the constant evolution of the digital era is the ideal one for an architecture that would maintain the quality of all its aspects over time as well as defining a set of clear objectives.

To exemplify this issue, I shall refer to what we call 'sustainable architecture':

For a time this term was used to refer to the inclusion of mechanisms whose purpose is to exploit alternative forms of energy. Nonetheless, commitment to the environment requires a vision of the future that begins with appropriate use of the resources of a specific place, in terms of orientation, command of sunlight, exploitation of natural light and so on, as well as use of materials that minimise the impact of transport and behave suitably in all senses (in their quality of definition of space, in their capacity to regulate temperature and, needless to say, in their long-term performance). I refer to a system of actions that must be implicit in what we understand as good architecture rather than a label that is added independently.

Of particular importance at present are two issues that represent society's becoming aware of the unsustainability of human activity in the developed countries: applied ethics and social responsibility.

Both are geared towards marking guidelines in favour of the common good and constitute a call for good professional practice.

If Corporate Social Responsibility involves compulsory compliance with national and international legislation, whose existence reflects what current social demands are, applied ethics may be understood in terms of the requirements of life in society rather than of a set of principles that may be imposed on a given reality, that is, they require us to assess specific situations without losing sight of the principles and values of the corresponding social environment.

All this is applicable to our profession, with all the more reason given the nature of its object.

Listening to society does not mean standing on the sidelines; it means making the effort to reflect on what we understand as 'good architecture'. As Mies said, '*I don't want to be interesting, I want to be good*'.

I should like to think that the new phase that is beginning after this latest edition, which marks the success of the first twenty-five years in the life of the Prize and during which over 2,500 works have been selected from all over Europe representing the richness and integration of its constituent cultures, will be disposed towards acknowledging efforts to combine new technologies with good practice in design and construction and addressing the impact – both positive and negative – that globalisation might have on the evolution of national architectures.

And returning to Mies's words, with which I opened this address:

'The new times are here with us; they exist regardless of whether we want them or not. [...]
The only decisive thing is how to assert ourselves in these given circumstances [...]
This is where the problems of the spirit begin. The important question is not "what" but "how".
[...] it is precisely the question of values that is decisive. We must build new values [...]
Because the correct and significant of all times –including the new times– is this: to provide the spirit with the opportunity to exist.' [3]
Mies van der Rohe

3. Closing address at the Vth *Deutscher Werkbund* congress held in Vienna in June 1930.

Reading European Architecture

Diane Gray

Coordinator,
Mies van der Rohe
Award

Since 1988, the architectural community across Europe has worked together to make the European Union Prize for Contemporary Architecture - Mies van der Rohe Award happen every two years. In looking back we can see that the Prize has been a way to record the construction of Europe over the last couple of decades. At the same time it has been a mechanism by which to gather together and make public the ideas, doubts and debates that have been behind this period of prolific production by European architects.

So it seemed that the best way to go about making a book to celebrate the Prize's 25th anniversary was to rely on the protagonists who have been involved in the award process from the beginning – the institutions, professionals and the projects themselves – to tell this story. Quite simply, the Prize would never have made it to here without their participation.

But first let's make a sketch of how it all started, and in order to do so it's necessary to go back another five years, that is to 1983 when the reconstruction of Mies van der Rohe's Barcelona Pavilion had just gotten under way. Understanding the history of this small building on Montjuïc is a way of understanding much of European history in the last century. Built for the 1929 International Exhibition, it was the scenario for the meeting of the Weimar authorities and the Spanish King at the exhibition opening. Demolished shortly after the closing of the exhibition, the Pavilion was absent during the tragic conflicts that took place across Europe in the years to come.

It only reappeared again in the 1980s, in a newly democratic situation, when the Barcelona City Hall decided to rebuild it on its original site. Oriol Bohigas, as the head of urbanism and the architects in charge of the project – Ignasi de Solà-Morales, Cristian Cirici and Fernando Ramos – all played key roles in the reconstruction along with Arthur Drexler, who made available MoMA's Mies van der Rohe archive.

Meanwhile, the idea for a European architecture award, for which the Pavilion was to be the symbol, was proposed to the European Parliament by member Xavier Rubert de Ventós. In 1987, just under a year after the reconstruction of the Pavilion was completed, the agreement was signed by European Commissioner Carlo Ripa di Meana and Barcelona Mayor Pasqual Maragall to launch the 'Mies van der Rohe Award of the European Communities'. To this day, the sculpture that the prize winners receive is a sculpture by artist Xavier Corberó based on the columns of the Barcelona Pavilion.

The framework for the Prize's objectives and organisation has been adapted over time, but the basic ideas have remained the same. From the beginning it has been a process focused on collaboration, which can be seen in the different phases of each award cycle.

The first step is the nomination phase. A group of experts nominate the projects to be considered by the jury. These professionals – architects, critics, professors, and curators – are asked to submit proposals of works that have been completed in the previous two years (the exception to this timeframe was in the inaugural 1988 award when projects dating from 1984 were included).

This network of experts has been continuously expanding; in 1988 there were seventeen experts and in latest edition in 2013 there were more than sixty. In addition, the member associations of the Architects' Council of Europe ACE and the other national professional associations have also become part of the nomination network.

The institutions that form part of the Advisory and Steering Committees have played an essential role in the organisation. Representatives of these institutions have participated as consultants, experts who nominate works and as members of the jury.

With respect to the jury members, it was established from the very beginning that their job would be to review all the proposals of the nominators and to make the selection of a prize winner. However, two significant changes in terms of their tasks were added over the years.

For the fifth edition in 1996, it was decided that the jury members would formally decide upon five or so finalists, which they would visit before making their decision in a second meeting to be held immediately after the final site visit.

The other key modification has to do with the 'call for proposals' by the European Commission for the 'European Union Prize for Contemporary Architecture' that took place in 2001. The Fundació Mies van der Rohe submitted the model of the Mies van der Rohe Award including the Emerging Architect Special Mention that would highlight work by young professionals. The Mies van der Rohe Award model was accepted and from then on the two names became fused together and the selection of the special mention became part of the decision-making process by the jury.

One of the most important aspects that has remained the same from the first edition twenty-five years ago has been the jury's selection of a group of shortlisted works that are published in a catalogue and presented in a travelling exhibition that is shown during the year between each convocation.

It is in this broad selection of works, along with the complete list of nominees for each year, where we can see how Europe has been defining itself and its priorities through the wide-spread construction of schools, libraries, markets, hospitals, town halls, housing, police stations and museums. Successful architectural practice has always had to rely on a combination of talent and opportunity. In taking a look at the award database, where all the nominated projects are presented, one can see that during the past twenty-five years European architects have enjoyed a good measure of both resulting in public and private commissions that are in many cases the result of competitions.

At the same time, the incorporation of new countries has brought new architectures and new architects, has increased the complexity and enriched the contents by encouraging a wider debate on European architectural paradigms.

This book has been divided into three sections as a way to provide different levels of reading. First of all there is a photographic survey of the prize winners, finalists and shortlisted projects. Among other things, we can note how young architects who were part of the first selections have become central figures of the latest editions, in much the same way as the architects emerging today will surely be called on to be the central protagonists in the years to come.

Secondly, there is a collection of articles that have been written by the jury members from the first edition in 1988 to the latest edition in 2013. These are followed by five recent essays that reflect on the current situation, where we have been and where we might be going. The chronological reading of these texts transforms them into an articulated and continuous narrative about the development of theoretical and critical thinking in relation to European architecture. If the Prize is significant in the larger scheme of things it is because of its capacity to bring together reflections about the constructed landscape in order to formulate diverse ideas and discourses that can be relevant in confronting the many challenges we face.

The book closes with a timeline that walks through some of the major events of these last twenty-five years. It's a reminder of the huge changes that have taken place during this period and that architecture is the constructed vision of the social, cultural and economic history that we are creating everyday.

Photographic Survey

1988 — 2013

1988

1990

Kunsthaus Bregenz Peter Zumthor / Büro Peter Zumthor **Prize Winner**

Netherlands Embassy Berlin Rem Koolhaas, Ellen van Loon / OMA **Prize Winner**

Universiteit Utrecht

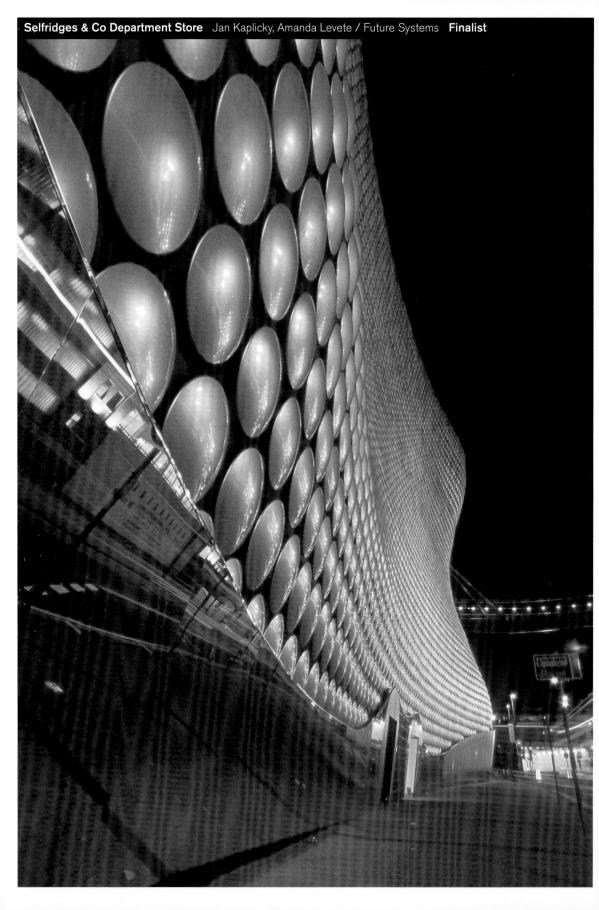

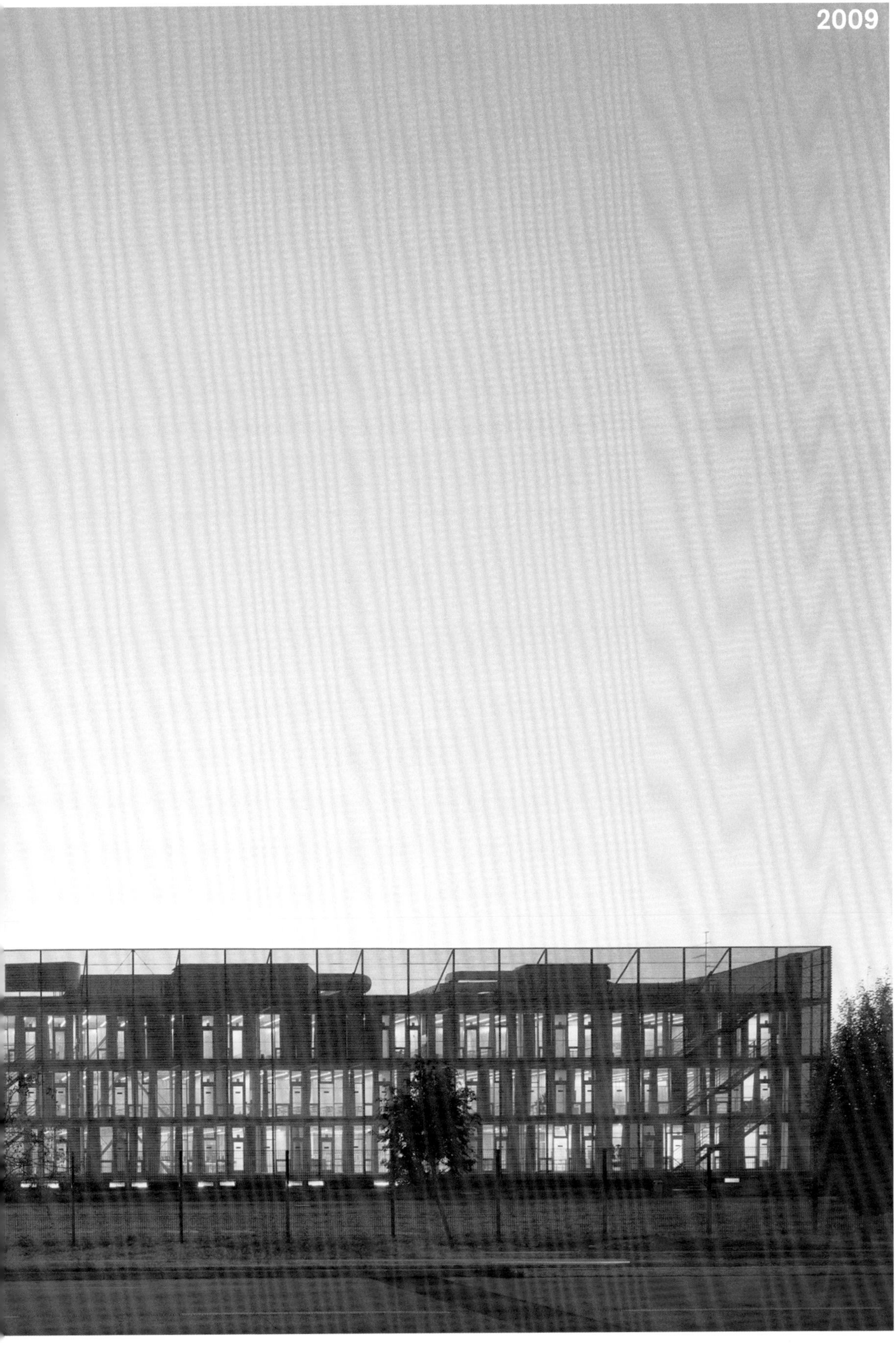

Essays

1988 – 2013

Retrospective Reflections on the Inauguration of the Mies van der Rohe Award

Kenneth Frampton

(1988)

Our idea of the modern is suffering a sea change; for nothing seems to be new in the sense that it once was. This is surely due to the constantly accelerating rate of change that increasingly renders every innovation obsolete before it has even had a chance to become fully assimilated. This rapid techno-economic change has disconcerting implications at many levels, not least of which is the apocalyptic transformation of the climate under the impact of world-wide consumerism. This emerging crisis has had implications for architecture for some time and in this regard the Mies van der Rohe Award may already be seen as compensating, at a relatively small cultural level, for the socio-ecological disruptions arising through the ever escalating expansion of megalopolitian urbanism. With the fall of the Berlin Wall in 1989 and the subsequent enlargement of the European Community, the destiny of Europe was challenged by a newly emergent condition in both an economic and a cultural sense.

While the inauguration of this award was situated at the threshold of a newly emergent Europe, it may also be regarded in retrospect as having been an unconscious response to the American Pritzker Prize for Architecture. At the same time, it cannot be simply seen as a reaction, for then, as now, it honours a very different cultural constituency. Thus, where the Pritzker is international in scope, the Mies van der Rohe Award seeks solely to encourage architectural excellence in Europe and with this it strives to further the spiritual identity and strength of the entire region. In the words of the inaugural conditions, the aim was to reinforce the concern of the EEC Commission for the survival of European urban culture, which was seen as having a chance to nurture its own tradition through exemplary modern works.

With this in mind, the first award jury was convened in June 1988 to select a single prize-winner out of some twenty-four nominees. This limited number of candidates was selected by seventeen appointed experts, representing between them what were then the member states of the EEC, with more than one expert nominating on behalf of some of the larger nations. While the jury itself could also nominate candidates for the award, it was nonetheless restricted to advancing the name of a single European architect as meriting the honour for a building erected in the EEC over the previous two years. Since this was the inaugural occasion, the time limit was somewhat extended at the jury's discretion in order to admit slightly older works that were judged as having made significant contributions to the European scene. This accounts for the jury's decision to award the inaugural Prize to Álvaro Siza for his Borges & Irmão Bank completed in Vila do Conde in 1986.

Although the jury arrived at a consensus about this uniquely distinguished work, it has to be acknowledged that among the shortlist there were many excellent examples of the different genres that then made up the spectrum of the emerging postmodern era, ranging from so-called high-tech works to buildings that evoked traditional forms. In the first cut the jury tried to select the best representatives of these different genres, thereby attempting to transcend, as far as it was possible, the more pluralistic aspects of style. While it is, by now, a somewhat obsolete exercise to classify all these different approaches by name, one may nonetheless still comment on the issues raised by certain buildings that were given particular consideration by the jury.

While recognising the risks entailed in indulging in any kind of ideological taxonomy, it is nonetheless remarkable how many of the nominated works fell into one class or other of what have since become more or less recognized genres. Thus, the stylistic spectrum of the works nominated at the time may be seen, in retrospect, as coming under such headings as *high-tech*, *neo-rationalist*, *contextualist*, *minimalist*, *structuralist* and *neo-historicist*. Some of these categories display more clearly identifiable characteristics than others and moreover, as always, subtle distinctions may invariably be found within the different expressions falling under the same rubric. Thus, while the works of the high-tech architects, namely, Richard Rogers, Norman Foster and Renzo Piano, all display to varying degrees the same concern for the overt expression of structure and for a level of detailing that directly reflects the mode of production, the specific role played by mechanical services in relation to the structure varies in each instance. So while they all ostensibly embraced the same techno-ethical code, it may be argued that where Rogers is exceptionally expressive at the level of services, Foster is the more measured with regard to the balance between structural and mechanical components, and Piano emerged, at the time, as the one architect who paid most attention to the micro-tectonics imposed by the means of production.

The works of the Neo-Rationalists, on the other hand, may be distinguished by the degree of their adherence to the normative plan typology, irrespective of whether the approach is somewhat technocratic, as in the case of Josef Paul Kleihues' Neukölln Hospital built near Berlin in 1986, or more metaphysical, as in the case of the works nominated on behalf of Oswald Mathias Ungers. With regard to this last I have in mind the complex that Ungers designed for the Frankfurt Trade Fair or, say, the Karlsruhe Regional Library or the Polar Institute that he designed for Bremen. Thus, we see how wide the variations were even within one generally accepted approach. While the young Mario Botta could then be unequivocally identified as a Neo-Rationalist, in other similar works of the time the evocation of classicism seemed to be too direct and one remained uncertain as to whether the buildings in question should be classified as Neo-Rationalist or Neo-Historicist. The works of Aldo Rossi seemed extremely ambiguous in this regard and one was aware at the time of a number of other architects who were formally of a late modern persuasion but who displayed a similar ambiguity. In many instances the nominations were strongly influenced by contextual considerations, as in the case of Gino Valle's Giudecca Housing in Venice of 1986 or Colquhoun and Miller's Whitechapel Art Gallery of 1985.

The boundary separating Neo-Rationalism from Neo-Historicism is at times so delicate as to enable one to see architects as passing almost imperceptibly from one category to the next. Riviere, Ortega and Capitel's reformulation of the Puerta del Sol in Madrid (1986) were clearly typical of this, as was Rossi's Funerary Chapel of 1987. Colquhoun and Miller's pedimented terrace housing also clearly crossed over towards historicism, as does James Stirling's gratuitous gravitation towards both traditional types details, as in his Wissenschaftszentrum completed in Berlin's Tiergarten in 1987. Similarly, for all their previous commitment to the modern tradition, the small bank built on Rhodes to the designs of the Antonakakis partnership, studio 66, in 1985 suffered from similar regressive tendencies, and much the same may be claimed for the corner infill block, built in Antwerp in 1988, to the designs of the Belgian AWG team.

Save for the exfoliating, electronically controlled sun screens of the Institut du Monde Arabe, there is nothing historicist about the Minimalism practised by Jean Nouvel. However, Nouvel was too technologically indulgent at the time to qualify as a rigorous Minimalist. His particular form of playful rhetoric favoured an uncommon combination of extravagant technical gestures with modest, expedient, off-the-peg, mass-produced components. Elsewhere a kind of Constructivist-Minimalism was advanced in different ways by the Austrian Gustav Peichl and by the Dutch architect Rem Koolhaas. Peichl's late Constructivism was influenced to an equal degree by Hans Poelzig's pre-war Expressionism and by Otto Wagner's tectonic precision, as one could find this at the time in his Phosphate Elimination Plant built in Berlin in the late 1980s. Koolhaas aspired to an altogether cooler, one might say dispensable modernity, as was evident in his Dance Theatre completed in The Hague in 1987, which was indifferently detailed. Where Koolhaas was preoccupied with a Neo-Suprematist, gestural approach to form and space, Peichl remained committed to the expressive potential of a precisely detailed technology down to the last bolt. The Plaça dels Països Catalans, built outside Sants station in Barcelona to the designs of Helio Piñón and Albert Viaplana in 1983, was, at the time, one of the most sublime works to be found in the Minimalist vein. The light techno-topographic manner of this urban set-piece put these architects into a class apart, although at times they also showed a certain affinity for the Aaltoesque organic manner of the Porto School.

Structuralism could then be seen as an approach that stressed the cellular generation of space along with its constructional articulation. This was an exclusively Dutch idiom profoundly influenced by Aldo van Eyck and represented among candidates for the award in the works of Theo Bosch and Herman Herteberger, by Bosch's Faculty of Arts for Amsterdam University of 1984 and by Hertzberger's Apollo Schools in Amsterdam of the same date. While Bosch's piece is an appropriate form of urban infill, reinforcing the existing street pattern by its scale and the street contained within the project itself, Hertzberger's buildings invariably attained a fusion of formal brilliance with a socio-anthropological potential that was hard to match. As

Hertzberger put it, 'I try to make my architecture appropriate in order that it may be appropriated.' The stepped central theatrical space of his Apollo schools is typical in this regard in that it served the school community in different ways, affording different kinds of experience according to the circumstances. Thus, it could be appropriated for the purposes of assembly or for theatrical performances, while in an everyday sense it could serve as a space of public appearance where children may casually meet, talk, sit or do their homework.

Moderate-income urban housing was then, at least, a particularly European achievement, and among some of the finest nominations submitted for the initial award were works of this genre and with respect to which mention should be made in retrospect of a number of successful examples, including Siza's reinterpretation of the Dutch housing tradition in the Schilderswijk, The Hague, which was exceptionally sensitive with respect to the type-form adopted and the continuity of the street fabric as opposed to the more monumental mega-urban pieces designed by Henri Ciriani, Henri Gaudin and Wilhelm Holzbauer.

At the time, it seems that the creative nexus of the European late modernism was most fully cultivated in the Iberian Peninsula from whence came works of exceptional quality from Seville, Barcelona, Madrid and Oporto and many other Spanish and Portuguese provincial cities. In this regard, much attention was paid by the jury to Rafael Moneo's Roman archaeological museum completed in Mérida in 1986, not only for the strength of its tectonic form, but also for its urban responsiveness and for its subtle approach to the history of the place. By audaciously recognising that not all archaic ruins are equally sacrosanct and that, as such, they ought to be integrated into our everyday life, Moneo was able to implant his museum over the excavations of the original Roman city, thereby establishing a dialogue between living walls and dead foundations. In so doing, he enabled visitors to walk quite literally between two realities, causing them to experience, as in a catacomb, something of the urban presence of the lost Roman past. Furthermore, by the judicious introduction of a tunnel, Moneo enabled one to pass from the nether world of the foundations to the ruins of two Roman amphitheatres situated on the nearby site. The concrete cross-walls of this museum were faced in a brick of Roman proportions, while the past also appeared in this work at a metaphorical level, engendering a number of typological and tectonic associations, ranging, say, from a medieval warehouse to a modern factory.

In a similar Iberian vein, attention was given by the jury to the works of the brilliant young Spanish engineer Santiago Calatrava, above all for his remarkable Bach de Roda-Felip II bridge, completed within the inner suburbs of Barcelona in 1987. Like Moneo's Mérida Museum, Calatrava's bridge was an object lesson in maximising the urban potential of a single structure, serving in this instance as an urban fix in terms of the road and rail approaches to the no-man's-land of the city's outskirts. At the same time, it functioned as a link between small public parks situated on either side of the rail line. One also registered in this regard the general Iberian prowess in the field of landscape as was evident in Barcelona, in the work of Martorell, Bohigas and Mackay, above all with respect to their Creueta del Coll Park, realised in 1987.

In granting the inaugural prize to Siza, the jury effectively honoured not only an exceptional work by a very distinguished architect but also the regional culture of which he was then, as now, the most prominent representative; the School of Porto, from which we received other nominations such as that of Siza's talented peer, Alcino Soutinho, and a house from the hand of his former assistant, Eduardo Souto de Moura, as well as a stadium that was then under construction in Braga to the designs of Gonçalo Byrne.

When one looks back over this inaugural event, nothing is more understandable in retrospect than the gap separating the oldest from the youngest of the architects preselected and nominated for the prize. And while we were presented with numerous works designed by architects in their mid-forties, the oldest architect pre-selected was Ignazio Gardella, who at eighty-four and after over half a century of practise was still capable of producing an impressive work and in fact, nothing was more moving among the nominations received for the prize than the funerary monument that Gardella realised in Brescia in 1985; an impressive exercise in precision brickwork displaying a maturity and a discipline are less common in the younger generation.

Kenneth Frampton is the Ware Professor of Architecture at Columbia University in New York. He was the Chair of the jury for the 1988 and 1990 awards. This essay from 1988, which was published in the first award catalogue has been revised by Kenneth Frampton for this publication.

Notes on the Second Prize

Vittorio Gregotti

(1990)

The conditions of the Mies van der Rohe Award for European Architecture are well known: a work of architecture is chosen from among those realised during the two years prior to the designation of the Award by a European architect in one of the countries belonging to the Community, and a group of works are pointed out as being worthy to appear as the best produced during the same biennium. The jury consists exclusively of architects and architecture historians, there being no bureaucratic presence alien to the discipline. By contrast to the celebrated Pritzker Prize, it is consequently not the career of a particular architect that is evaluated (although this factor has a major role to play when it comes to the debate), but rather a specific work. Excluded, therefore, are unrealised projects and project activity in the fields of urban design, planning and industrial product design, and works linked to restoration and activities such as constructional and urban restructuring, which in recent years have acquired both a major category as instruments and considerable quantitative weight. Limits remain uncertain as regards large-scale civil engineering works, bridges, dams, viaducts and infrastructures, which represent the highest economic investments made during the period and possibly the most important contributions (both positive and negative) to transformation of the European urban environment and landscape.

In the first edition the jury, presided over by Kenneth Frampton, awarded the Prize to the Borges e Irmão Bank in Vila do Conde (1986) by the Portuguese Álvaro Siza Vieira; in the second, the same jury designated the Prize to Norman Foster's Stansted Airport project for London. As the reader will appreciate, two designations in very different directions: the first, a work which once again promotes an architectural culture guided by poetic concerns linked to the subject of relationships with the context, with specific identity; the second, a work which confirms, equally poetically, the specific content of technological effort, making of this a mimesis of the values of an internationalist scientific-technical civilisation. The composite nature of the jury, the prevalence of a pluralist logic (with all the limitations and potential errors the term pluralism implies), and the very condition of architectural culture, marked as it is by a rather complex geography of changing positions – mannerism and eclecticism being recognisable in the architectural production of these years –, have led to such different results in the verdicts of the jury in these first two editions of the Prize.

However, there are other limits, constituted by the Prize rules themselves, which must be taken into account if a true evaluation is to be made of the results and the significance of these two editions. One of these limits is the restriction of the Prize to European architecture, especially in terms of the selection made of works to form the group judged to be the best architecture produced in the preceding biennium.

In the first place, a biennium is too short a period in which to conduct an analysis that proposes significant differences; although architectural practice has unfortunately approached the production of image, its specific, slow and collective ways of being remain in the long term structures, in solutions and perspectives, which impose a different rhythm on significant changes.

In the second place, the exclusion – determined by the Prize stipulations – of certain countries of great importance in the European architectural culture of these years, such as Switzerland, Austria, Sweden, Norway, Finland and the Eastern countries, means that the works selected form a very incomplete picture of European architectural culture.

Indeed, some of these excluded countries are in fact very good indicators of the research tendencies that characterise the profile of European architecture in relation to that of the rest of the world, and one need only consider the complexity and special identity of Austrian contributions of recent years, the quality of work in Italian-speaking Switzerland (the so-called Scuola del Ticino), the ingenuity and high intelligence of some Czechoslovakian groups or the special value placed on the interpretation of tradition in modern Finnish works to appreciate the truth of this. Despite these limitations, however, the group of works chosen may be regarded as indicative of certain interests, even on the basis of the exclusions which have been made.

For example, in the second edition of the Prize there was a surprising (and as far as I am concerned, fortunate) absence of what the newspaper critics would define as the 'postmodern', and no echo at all of what is being propagated as 'deconstructivism'. This fact indicates on the one hand that the postmodern craze is approaching its twilight and on the other, significantly, that the jury revealed a certain firmness and resolution in the face of excessively improvised and fleeting stylistic vogues. Furthermore, it is possible to recognise a just criterion which tends to exclude not only quantitative professionalism (even though it may be of a high level) but also the deliberately sought-after fantasy, research into the expressive effect for its own sake, and departures from the specific framework of the discipline itself.

After a long period in which there has been a trend towards contamination of languages, towards metaphorical interferences which have been reflected in the form of fragmentation and adherence to an aesthetic of opportunities, and towards acceptance of everyday congestion, there seems to be an emerging demand for a refocusing and for critical transparency linked to the tradition of significant construction. Similarly, in the rejection of all dual radicalism, developments seem to be taking place in awareness of the fact that modern projects, as critical rather than organic projects in relation to social institutions, do not meet structural demands: in other words, at the limits of the indispensable collaborationism, which since time immemorial has made the concrete realisation of architecture possible.

This optimistic judgment is undoubtedly more a hope than a promise; at the same time, however, it is true that the designations of this edition of the European Community Prize certainly do not contradict these hopes. Since European identity is rather like a confederation of differences, and the question of the dialectic between internationalism (of technologies, of communications, of powers) and local identity continues to be a debate which, though lively, is one of the most difficult to bring to a satisfactory conclusion, it is also crucial to make an evaluation of the different national contributions and how they are revealed in the works chosen.

The first thing we notice is the reappearance in national cultures of regional identities and differences which endow the picture of relations and influences with complexity. A thoroughly valid example here is that of Spain, whose coherence in terms of quality projects is, in my opinion, due totally to the articulation not only of the different generations but also, and above all, to that of the different production centres. The Barcelona-Madrid bipolarity (with clear predominance of the importance of the first for many years) has been replaced by a policentrality, from the Seville School to the centres situated around Basque culture, and from Murcia to the Catalan provinces, which has given rise to a new wealth of ideas and realisations.

To this should be added a policy of exceptional events, such as the Seville EXPO or the Barcelona Olympics, and in general the options adopted for the launching of the democratic reconstruction of the country which marked the 1980s and the results of which are now becoming visible.

For opposite reasons, France and Portugal represent different cases. In France, the resolutions of a determined central policy of initiatives have radically changed the level of maturity of the country's architecture. In particular it has been the public entity which, under its own initiative, has fostered architecture as one of the most significant expressions of the state and of society. Only twenty years ago, after the death of Le Corbusier, French architecture was in a deplorable state of neglect. Today there are at least ten French architects of quality – whose work perhaps reveals an excess of deliberately artistic conduct – and the competitions organised there, more numerous than in the rest of Europe, are also the most open, since they are public competitions situated on different levels of complexity and territorially distributed, according to a policy designed to offer major opportunities to the young.

It does not matter if the evaluation of some of the regime's *Grands Travaux* is not a positive one; the results of attention to architectural culture (as in the fields of history, of communication, of exhibitions, of books) have been obtained thanks to the support of a functionarial structure of the State and of local administrations, with all their traditional efficiency.

On the other hand, what has emerged in Portugal is a genuinely 'autochthonous' school of architecture with unitary methods and principles that produce solutions rich in diversity, since they are able to find the truth of each specific case and transform it into the project's guiding material. The country's small number of architects often construct in conditions of poverty and precariousness; yet they are endowed with an exceptional poetic talent when it comes to determining the most intimate and specific dimensions of a territory and of a whole country. As the reader well knows, Portugal is at present a developing country and we do not know how this development will be in the future, whether the qualities created will be enjoyed, or whether the architects themselves will be capable of making the necessary qualitative leap in order to face the problems ensuing from this development. Nevertheless, the undeniable fact is that the premises with which to confront development and architectural quality are in the forefront of the most serious part of the discipline.

The situation in Great Britain is more problematical: a recession in the field of construction development has been followed by the reappearance of a neostylistic conservative resistance: to be honest, quite justified by a considerable number of unfortunate cases, but often disastrous for the best architects. While alongside figures of great stature such as Foster, Colquhoun, Stirling, Rogers and others, a series of excellent younger architects like Chipperfield and Armstrong are emerging, and there is an all-pervading feeling of disorientation which produces either an architecture-spectacle built upon fragmentation and the metaphor of visual languages, or else something efficiently planned as the operative arm of the promoter.

A case apart is Holland, where architects such as van Eyck or Hertzberger represent in quite different ways a specific national tradition, while for his part Koolhaas sets out to affirm the internationalisation of problems and solutions, the importance of replies to issues of horizontal congestion, and the value of provisionality and fragmentation. The younger generation, numerous and well trained, is divided among these different interpretations and often alternates between them.

The most important lesson to be learnt from Denmark (beyond the totally fortuitous case of von Spreckelsen) is still the great civic quality of the country's realisations, a quality born especially from discretion and concern for collective well-being: a crucial lesson in these times of voracious destruction of established rules.

Tombazis, Atonakakis and Valsamakis are the three Greek architects whose work has achieved greatest consolidation. However, there is also now an interesting group of youngsters in Greece - many of whom have trained in England at the Architectural Association - whose mouthpiece is the journal *Tefchos*; not to be forgotten either is the task of establishing relations with international culture begun by Elia Zenghelis.

The presence of few works of Italian and German architecture among those selected is by no means representative of the international weight of these architectures, and this for a number of reasons. In the case of Italy, this situation reflects current difficulties to be faced in the country, above all of an institutional nature consisting in the minor importance of representation attached to architecture by public entities and the State, inefficiency when it comes to following up programmes and in the poor conditions of an overcrowded university. However, this does not mean that in Italy only the five or six internationally recognised architects can work. On the contrary, a wide and varied group of young and considerably talented architects is now emerging, such as Francesco Venezia, Guido Canali, Michele Reginaldi, Franco Purini, Pasquale Culotta, Romano Burelli and others perfectly able to continue making important contributions from Italy to the world of architectural culture, from reflections on the city and on the territory – essential project materials – to those on history and memory, going back even to the mid-1950s; and from subjects referring to knowledge of and preservation of historical cities to critical analysis of the crisis of Modernity.

As regards German architecture, for purely circumstantial reasons some of the best architects, such as Ungers and Kleihues or the younger figures Brandt, Kollhoff and Dudler, have not been well represented. Above all, however, it must be remembered that the questions that German architecture must face at the moment – with the reunification of the country symbolically represented by the problems related to Berlin – had yet to arise in 1988/90, the two-year period from which the works have been selected.

All these issues expect a major contribution from European architecture towards solving essential problems linked to the construction of the European city of the 1990s and, in this context, the Mies van der Rohe Award for European Architecture may have a critically orientative role to play.

Vittorio Gregotti, a principal of Gregotti Associati in Milan and professor at the Università Iuav di Venezia, was a member of the jury for the 1988 and 1990 editions of the Prize.

Dilemmas of European Architecture

Ignasi de Solà-Morales

(1994)

Kenneth Frampton's selection of works for this exhibition is based on those chosen by the jury members in the first four editions of the Mies van der Rohe Award for European Architecture, and therefore covers practically the whole of this last decade of architectural production in the EEC countries.

The apparent diversity of the works might lead, at first glance, to the belief that both a common style and a predominant tendency are lacking. Nonetheless, I am convinced this effect is largely misleading and that, in fact, the European production of recent years reveals a considerable number of common denominators which, I feel sure, will make it perfectly locatable in space and time once our sight has recovered from the distorting effects of the close-up.

Today, more than ever before, exchanges are constant and what is being done in Italy, England or Portugal becomes known and divulged elsewhere extremely quickly. Architecture is a powerful instrument of communication and interrelationships are permanent. We read the same journals, listen to the same lectures, contemplate images by the same photographers and publish the same critical texts. Furthermore, awarding prizes allows people both in Europe and all over the world to become rapidly familiar with new European work.

This cultural space still retains its capacity for experimentation while, despite its fragile institutional support, the economic and political phenomenon of the European Community is nevertheless a reality in process.

While much of Europe has an increasing number of elements in common, traditions and local histories, languages and landscapes still mark differences. Consequently, between ourselves I believe that nowhere else in the world are cities so distinct from each other: Paris is not Milan, London is not Berlin and Oporto is not Amsterdam. Strong tensions between opposing interests and passions pervade Europe to the extent that what might be taken as characteristic traits of the present situation should be seen as dilemmas rather than as points in common.

Although it is evident that recent European production, of which this exhibition is an anthology, is representative of the most self-searching and critical trends in the whole of world architecture, it is nonetheless equally true that this work does not always provide an accurate reply to clearly defined problems. More than any other architecture, that of Europe lives on the knife's edge between constant antitheses, so that not only its interest, but also its limits, can be found in the constant paradoxes revealed in individual works.

As architecture it is neither potent, nor great, nor ostentatiously tendentious. On the contrary, its greatest strength lies in the constant tensions between those created and the never-ending search for a *coincidentia opositorum* that can never be resolved.

The ambiguous relationship between architecture and the technics that build it constitutes not the first principle but the first of the dilemmas we must point out here. The modern-movement tradition absorbed technology into machinism to form a conceptual assembly explicable in terms only of the far more advanced state of the mechanical world compared to forms of construction. It was a decisive conceptual displacement within what Giedion described as the mechanisation that takes command. For the first time in the West, architecture was looked upon as primordially mechanical instead of statically tectonic, as in the classical tradition. Once faith in and enthusiasm for the fundamental concepts of modern architecture have been lost, this is a conflict which remains permanently open.

In the last ten years, renewed attention to the technical expression of architectural objects has reawakened awareness of the problem. Most of the works presented in this selection are caught between mechanical confidence as a metaphor of modern technical civilisation and the constant winks of complicity that undermine this very confidence. For the more literally minded Neo-Modernists, more in line with the mechanicist sensitivity that permeates the whole of 20th-century architecture, these aspects of present-day architecture must be potentiated anew.

Norman Foster, Jean Nouvel and Renzo Piano would basically be followers of this line. Their mechanicism, however, is neither crude nor naïve. Their architecture is built up by successive layers, by attention to problems which cannot be solved exclusively by applying the mechanical analogy. Theirs are predominantly machinist exaltations, enthusiasm for the values of accurate adjustment, of tension, of repetitive production outside the work, of the rhetoric of assembly. The umbrella-shaped module that forms the roof of Stansted Airport, for example, is as precise in appearance as the assembled parts of a bicycle. Everything seems measured and tightly fitting. Here, however, there is nostalgia for the column and the architrave unmistakably present in the timid hints of definition of the base, the shaft and the capital.

There are other silent technologisms, tense but stable, such as the strand of Neo-Miesianism that runs through the work of some Minimalists. In the case of Souto de Moura, López Cotelo and Carlos Puente, Christer and Harðardóttir, and Hertzberger technologism is received in nuanced form thanks to the fact that a great architect digested the problem when it first emerged. The Miesian road to technology is a merciful and comforting solution. Intelligence and good taste have reduced the terms of the conflict to the minimum, converting them into an elegant gesture. However, in the Miesian tradition the dilemma subsists in that, on the one hand, it rejects naïve mechanism and, on the other, is governed by the categorical imperative of recognising technics as the basis of modern architecture and culture.

At the other extreme of the dilemma we find the imperfect machines. They are the unproductive, celibate motors which, since the time of Duchamp and Picabia, are in the thoughts and minds of Modernity. An unproductive machine is the embodiment of paradox; it is also, however, an act of rebellion. To mistrust the machine, surrender oneself to the dream of the impossible machine, celebrate the breakdown and the imprecision and gratuitousness of desires is also a recurring position in the European cultural tradition.

The machines by Peichl, Tschumi, Koolhaas, Miralles and Pinós or Zenghelis and Sauerbruch are basically absurd. They constitute a subtle parody of machinism to be interpreted in a surrealist sense. At this extreme, demands made upon architecture by machinist culture are met through either irony or impotence.

The Braun factory by Stirling and Wilford, in collaboration with Walter Nageli, is the best example of the celibate machine. A posthumous work by the Great Conjuror, it is also an early work by an intelligent partner who has managed to add to Stirlingian perplexities a far more precise sense of pluralism. While in his last works Stirling publicly dynamited his own ideas, what he reveals in the Braun factory is the impossibility of recomposing the form of an industrial building with a single technique, a single machine.

Superimposed upon the dilemma of machinism is the dilemma of signs. The whole of European architecture is weighed down by the burden of its own culture. It is difficult to avoid one's sight becoming impregnated with icons from a wide variety of provenances. In other cultural areas, the world of signs originates possibly in ambits other than that of architecture. Such would seem to be the situation in the United States or Japan. If we overlook the banality of what is known as Postmodern Historicism, it is undeniably true that today's European architects cannot erase from their memories either Le Corbusier, Mies, Asplund and Terragni or Roman, Gothic and neo-classical architecture.

Even the greatest cultural sophistication generally embodied in European architecture is a prison from which it is difficult to escape. The liberty with which it is possible to manipulate signs, and the diversity of vocabularies within licit reach, do not appear to offer clear assistance in the search for limpid expression of architectural themes.

Constant metonymic operations appear in the word plays that architects are so reluctant to abandon. Perhaps in more innovative cultural contexts, things say what they are and signs clearly reflect what constitutes their meaning. In the intricate network of European architecture, however, it is unlikely that we shall find fundamentally univocal languages.

What does Rafael Moneo's Mérida Museum talk about? About Rome, medieval architecture, industrial architecture, a museum which is also a storehouse, a brick factory reminiscent of great Piacentinian constructions? So many possible readings coexist, each as licit as the others, that multiplicity of meanings seems to be one of the main objectives of a work of this kind. The same appraisal would be valid for Álvaro Siza's Borges e Irmão Bank. What is it that fascinates us about this tiny building standing so fragile in a part of the city that is neither particularly consistent nor well-defined? A prodigious dance of figures swirls around us when we contemplate the work through the eyes of architectural memory. We are astonished, fascinated when we appreciate the delicious dance of references being performed in its interior spaces. Perhaps there is no literal imitation; perhaps it cannot be said with certainty where each element comes from. But when we look at the bank building, we witness a procession in which Mies and Aalto, Asplund, Rietveld and Melnikov, together with Terragni, Távora and Albini pass before our eyes. The same phenomenon occurs in the work of Adolfo Natalini, in that of Alan Colquhoun and John Miller, and in that of Henri Ciriani, as well as in the aforementioned project by Stirling and Nageli and in the work of Souto de Moura, Ungers, and Zenghelis and Sauerbruch.

Fortunately, the postmodern whirlwind under its most commercial guise is absent from this exhibition. It is no less true, however, that the labyrinth of signs, the gratuitousness of their use and their clear availability are not a characteristic feature of commercial architecture only. Linguistic pluralism is founded on the absence of clear values honestly presented as unequivocal. The real situation is, by contrast, that European architecture has much, possibly too much, memory. The ghosts of its past are in the present, so that planning and building involve exorcising these ghosts and establishing, in each case, an interplay between their presence and their absence.

'The assessment of the impact of architecture on the development of European cities' is one of the objectives that justify the two-yearly prize awarded by the EEC through the Mies van der Rohe Foundation in Barcelona. This is a third dilemma that besets the best of today's European architecture. More than in any other part of the world, in Europe the city is the inevitable recipient of architecture. A recipient formed from the accumulation of experiences and from the successive decanting of operations carried out over the centuries. Unlike elsewhere in the world, in Europe architecture is required to be urban. This undoubtedly poses a problem, and it is for this reason that architecture's call to urbanity cannot be reflected obviously as a clear request that must be satisfied, but rather as a true agony.

Architects make cities, but architecture must respond to the city that has already been made and must continue to be made. The reader will understand that this is not exactly a simple demand on the part of traditionalism, contextualism or other ways of settling debts with history and with what already exists. It is equally true, however, that in Europe the requirement that architecture be coherent, receptive, constructive and respectful towards the city cannot be overlooked when it comes to raising a building *ex novo*. Recent theories on the site, *genus loci*, morphology, typology and so on have attempted to find ways to mediate between the existing urban fabric and the new architecture to come. More recent perceptions tend to privilege the other side of the coin by emphasising the innovatory obligation of every architectural act and the inevitable violation of what already exists perpetrated by all new architecture.

Between the extremes, but within and not on the fringe, of this dilemma, recent European architecture seems obliged to provide a specific reply, in each particular case, to demands which, on the other hand, architectural culture would consider unacceptable. Bonell and Rius's Badalona pavilion adopts this question as one of the crucial themes in its architectural definition. While evidently the technological and linguistic dilemmas are also present here, in this project it is the urban problem that takes the leading role.

This same leading role is equally evident in the Parc de la Creueta del Coll by MBM and in the Santa Justa Station by Cruz and Ortiz, as it is in the works of Carrilho da Graça, Tschumi, Behnisch, Colquhoun and Miller, Michel Kagan and, of course, in Gino Valle's Giudecca housing project. In all these projects there are references and attention to the city, both existing and future, both the city whose urban values need to be upgraded and the city which, above all, demands respect.

At the present moment, it is also possible to detect in Europe a neo-American strand which exalts indiscriminate juxtaposition, the conflict between architectural acts, and urban *laissez-faire*. The selection exhibited here reveals the extent to which, in Europe, any wildcat unloading of ideas, ways of operating, and utterly spontaneous rhetoric is immediately caught in the net of architectural and urban culture and prevented from travelling further unless it pays the toll of our own cultural tradition's concept of urbanity. To combat the mass import of models and images, our tradition has implemented policies of dissuasion born from analysis and methodical questioning.

These are the confines of European architectural culture. Its dilemmas. To reach their limits and to make the effort of measuring itself against them is this culture's most powerful form of expression.

A professor at the Escola Tècnica Superior d'Arquitectura de Barcelona, Ignasi de Solà-Morales (1942-2001) was a jury member for the first four editions of the Prize. This essay was published in the catalogue of the exhibition *European Architecture 1984-1994*, which was curated by Kenneth Frampton.

A New Simplicity:

Reflections on Architecture at the Turn of the Millennium

Vittorio Magnago Lampugnani

(1994)

Towards the close of the 19th century, the world of architecture saw a parade of virtually every known style pass by in increasingly rapid succession. It was an eclectic architectural jamboree in which elements of every era were flung together in picturesque layers and collages. Only once this orgy of unfettered historicism had reached a peak did a new counter-movement begin to emerge. Isolated at first, it began to distance itself radically from the prevailing stylistic potpourri, propagating simplicity as an economic, ethical and aesthetic ideal, and heralding the emergence of the Modern Movement, whose social and artistic triumph was to culminate in the Neue Sachlichkeit of the 1920s.

Today, as we approach not only the turn of a century but also a new millennium, something very similar seems to be happening. Once again, we find a jumble of different styles and fashions jostling for attention. Once again, we find ourselves reaching the point where there is no choice but to jettison the ballast accumulated in the course of a hundred years. Once again, simplicity would appear to offer the solution, albeit a rather different kind of simplicity from that which prevailed around 1900.

Let us take a step back in time. Architecture has never been a mere question of style. As a practical art which has to meet specific needs, it is inextricably linked to the prevailing lifestyle of the day. It is an expression of its time. But what can and should architecture express today?

Though we would do well to take stock of our present situation, it is hardly comforting. Philosophy, the one discipline which, through the ages, has stood aloof from the banality of everyday life, providing us with a guideline for living, has been pushed into a marginal position. Religion, its authority undermined, remains fossilised in its own rediscovery. The great ideologies, together with the political systems they once supported, have crumbled. The body politic no longer has anything to do with the science, let alone the art, of governing a people on the basis of law. Instead, it has come to be regarded as a shabby and rather superfluous crust which is, at best, tolerated. The economy, which has suffered bankruptcy in the so-called socialist countries to an extent no burgeoning capitalism could save, is moving into a recession that looks set to last a long time. Technology, left more or less to its own devices, has come up with an overwhelming number of inventions which are revolutionising our lives, particularly in the fields of telecommunications and genetic biology, yet our planet, boundlessly exploited for thousands of years, is teetering on the brink of ecological disaster. Like the nation states, the fine arts are fragmenting into a Babel of confusion, reflecting the utter lack of consensus in our society.

Needless to say, in the field of architecture, the situation is no different. Even if we ignore the sheer chaos prevailing in much of the building sector, in which architects themselves have little share, we find that architecture offers us small consolation. Its attempts to come to terms with a world which seems to be out of joint are as manifold as they are helpless.

Postmodernism is one such attempt. It emerged towards the end of the 1970s and sought to evade the aesthetic and moral dictatorship of Modernism by the use of historic references; buildings positioned in a way that would create new urban spaces, designed in a way that would enter into dialogue with the adjacent buildings, decorated in a way that would project a lively, varied and at times even witty appearance.

Yet for all this, the postmodernists, so hastily and enthusiastically applauded, tended to forget that most of the characteristics they claimed for their architecture were ill suited to the purpose. A joke told once too often soon grows stale. Witty architecture, if we have to look at it day in and day out, can soon get on our nerves. What started out as a jovial approach to building soon froze in an unbearable grimace. What should have been speaking architecture soon became a chattering architecture of grating repetitiveness. What is more, this new fashion quickly blazed a trail into every village and soon even the most petty bourgeois home boasted a broken arch and a colourful pillared portal. Even the masterpieces of great post-modern architecture with their contradictions between modern building techniques and historicising stone facades, already seem strangely outdated.

They were overtaken, at least in the specialist press and the arts sections of the daily papers, by the Deconstructivism which began to emerge in the 1980s. The deconstructivists, with an eye on the cryptic philosophy of uncertainty propagated by Jacques Derrida and Jean Baudrillard, could see at a glance that the world in which they were living was bent on rushing headlong towards self-destruction. It was precisely this that they sought to reflect in architecture, not without some profound soul-searching. Their bizarrely disjointed buildings with sharply angled slopes looked like some gigantic game of jackstraws, about to topple or collapse.

In fact, the comparison could often be taken rather more literally than the originators of the transitory (de-)construction might have wished. After all, first and foremost architecture is about creating sheltered spaces and, in order to construct such spaces, it is advisable, for rather obvious reasons of stability, to use simple (and immovable) vertical walls and supports. If they are placed at an angle, they tend to do exactly what they look as though they might do: collapse. Luckily, relatively few deconstructivist buildings actually did fall down, but in order to ensure that they kept standing, they often required such complex and costly reinforcement that most of them remained in the place where they were likely to do the least physical or financial harm: on the drawing board. What is more, their philosophical and aesthetic claim to visualise breakdown and fluidity was destroyed by the uncontrolled urban sprawl of our cities. Even the most skilfully staged scene of devastation seems almost twee when juxtaposed with similar but quite unintentional scenes of devastation. In a world already sinking into chaos, the effect of artificial chaos tends to seem more reassuring than shocking.

Such subversive intentions are entirely alien to the third major trend in contemporary architecture, which upholds the tenets of classical Modernism. Its representatives look back nostalgically to the 1920s when their heroes, Le Corbusier, Walter Gropius and Mies van der Rohe prevailed. Their keenest wish is to pursue and perfect their maxims. So much optimism in an age like ours seems suspicious to say the least. Indeed, what can be salvaged into the 1990s from the architectural achievements of 1920s Modernism can be little more than form alone. A villa by Richard Meier or a high-rise by Norman Foster may be beautiful, but they hardly represent our age. They are too elegant, too smooth, too airy, too futuristic for that. In short, they are too optimistic.

At least the turn to Modernism points towards an escape from the unbearable alternative between Postmodernism and Deconstructivism, between the populism pandering to taste and the arrogance of *épater le bourgeois*, between posturing affectation and a chamber of horrors. It is the path of neutrality. It eschews both Postmodernism's artificial proximity to life and the permanent irritation of Deconstructivism. Indeed, it stops insisting upon doing what architecture can never quite avoid anyway: teaching by dint of its presence alone. It reduces this teaching to a minimum. It is this that makes it, to some extent at least, humane.

Admittedly, these three main trends merely outline the rough triangulation of a cultural landscape which, in its infinite complexity, contains dozens of other trends besides. They break down what was, until around the mid-18th century, a more or less monolithic discipline, creating a confusing welter of seeming alternatives which purportedly embody some ominous democratic pluralism, while in fact embodying the dictatorship of arbitrariness. Neo-Modernism counters this with a sense of security drawn from recent history.

This alone, however, is not enough to mark the turn of an era; it has to go hand in hand with a change of paradigm. The first thing this change has to include is a return to simplicity. It has already been demanded. The reasons are many and varied. There are ideological reasons: in a world to be distributed as justly as possible amongst an increasing number of inhabitants, there can and should be no place for superfluity. There are technical reasons: if the production process is to be simplified in order to produce goods (including houses) en masse and more cheaply, everything that complicates these goods must be jettisoned. Finally, the reasons are aesthetic: since the advent of the industrial revolution, the simplification necessitated by the new social and technical needs has been ennobled by progressive culture and exalted to an artistic principle. In other words, we are no longer in a position to find pomp and circumstance pleasing, preferring instead the clear, the reduced and the uncluttered. Even the artificial variety which has become synonymous with humanity in the language of the petty bourgeoisie is no longer bearable. Why, if the row of offices aligned behind them is identical, should the windows not be identical too? Monotony is often more honest and more appropriate than variation for its own sake, which merely presents an illusion of difference where in fact there is none.

Second, however, simplicity and uniformity need not be the direct result of mindless economy. On the contrary, simplicity should involve a concentration of riches, a sublimation of complexity. Architecture, after all, depends upon so many factors: ideology, politics, money, technology. It also depends to some extent on the local building regulations, on the whim of the client and on the availability of materials. Of course, it depends, too, on how the building is used and its changing functions. All these factors have to be taken into account in a building in accordance with the concept of the person responsible for the design. Such a wealth of simplicity calls for hard work, patience and perseverance. Yet in the end, it has to look as though it had been executed effortlessly. Just as Michelangelo claimed for sculpture, it should look as though one had taken back all the effort invested in the work.

199

Third, one of the most irritating evils of our day and age is noise in the widest possible sense. In an era in which we are incessantly bombarded with sounds and images, architecture has to take a stance against such bombardment: it should be a place where our eyes can rest, a symbol of contemplation, the reification of silence. Once again, that means simplicity, clarity, uniformity. However, it also means discarding unnecessary multilayered facades and rejecting coldly mirrored glass surfaces or shimmering media hoardings in favour of sober plaster or stone walls, symbolising solidity and exuding an air of calm.

Fourth, our world is indubitably a world of ever-increasing chaos. Instead of simply presenting or even adding to the chaos, it must be stopped and reduced. Chaos does not make us feel at home in the world. In order to feel at ease, people need the same geometric order that the body exemplifies and the mind abstracts and develops. Because of its high-profile visibility and its longevity, architecture is destined to stand as an island of order in a torrent of chaos. A novelist does not write in order to show life as it is, but in order to suggest – by whatever detours he deems fit – the way it should be. An architect who is more than just the willing accomplice of politicians or developers does not build a house to make it fit in with the world, but to set an example. That means creating values he believes in and represents.

Fifth, architecture need not involve constant fundamental renewal. A love of innovation for its own sake is one of the most fateful inheritances of the avant-garde era. In those days, against the backdrop of the unwieldy academic approach of the 19th century, it was felt that whatever was not new was worthless.

Today, the very opposite is the case: far too much of what we have is new. And far too much of what is new has no reason to be new. Incessant change impedes the course of patiently improving on the achievements of the past, and hinders the fundamental consolidation of one's own achievements. Until the 18th century, architecture involved making tiny and barely perceptible improvements to that which already existed. Today, it would appear to consist of radically changing whatever exists, irrespective of whether or not that means improvement. We must renounce the myth of innovation as an independent value and apply it only where it is really necessary. Resigned as such an attitude may sound, it is the greatest conceivable challenge to us today. In this day and age, it takes far more courage, talent and energy to assert something conventional than it does to propagate the unconventional. The obvious is the greatest provocation.

Sixth, architecture which is not, as Mies van der Rohe sardonically remarked, 'reinvented every Monday morning', is also enduring architecture. It is the very opposite of a fashionable dress one wears just once or twice before relegating it to the back of the wardrobe after a few weeks because it has lost its fascination. Although the mechanism of urban economies leads to a rapid sequence of demolition and reconstruction, this is economically unacceptable and is unlikely to continue even in the private sector. Each building represents not only something of enormous value, but also a potential dumping ground. In an era of shrinking resources and increasing environmental pollution, we shall soon be unable to afford this kind of additional waste.

There is a seventh factor. An architecture of simplicity, density and silence, an architecture that is ordered, conventional and enduring, demands one indispensable ingredient if it is to avoid the pitfall of mere banality: it demands precision. A kaleidoscope of forms and colours, a short-lived expressiveness, need not pay much attention to detail. By contrast, reduction, condensation, succinctness and simplicity require precision. In the turmoil of the grotesque, lack of precision goes unnoticed. Discretion makes it inexorably visible. The architecture of new simplicity places small details in the foreground once again: how is the stone quarried and cut, the plaster mixed and applied, the window profiled? Small details these may be, minor or even secondary they certainly are not. It is precisely small details that have been the very essence of great architecture down the ages, from the Parthenon of Ictinus, Callicrates and Phidias to the Neue Nationalgalerie in Berlin designed by Ludwig Mies van der Rohe.

Seven demands for a new architecture: are they really necessary? Apparently, it would be neither exaggeration nor nostalgia to say that, in the course of the century which is now coming to an end, we have forgotten how to build houses properly. Anyone who can afford to do so lives in a renovated old building. That has nothing whatsoever to do with sentimentality; it is the perfectly understandable flight from those shabby, faceless entrance halls with their yellowing pot plants, their narrow stairways of polished artificial stone, their flimsy doors with the light aluminium door-handles, their low ceilings covered in woodchip paper, their thin walls, their poorly proportioned windows with the clumsy profiles (which, as though in compensation, can be turned and tilted any way we please) and their charmless cheap flooring. It is a flight from the world of plastic, from the painted concrete ground course and the silicone joints. It is a flight from the appalling architectural quality of contemporary housing.

Are we to believe, as we are told, that they are the way they are quite simply because they are new? Our construction industry, our system of standards and our economy permit nothing else. They force us into shabby mediocrity. The recession is unlikely to improve the situation.

It is true that the economic situation is not getting any better. It is true that less money is available for construction. It is also true that we are going to have to build more, rather than less housing, at any rate. It is inevitable that our standards will have to be lowered. This does not mean that we have to lower the quality as well. Standards can be lowered and quality increased at the same time, as many an old farmhouse testifies impressively. Of course, architecture is invariably part and parcel of a political, normative and economic context. Yet within that context, it can and must become an instance that sets its own priorities and prefigures a new development.

Already, the first tentative steps are being taken in this direction. They are, as we might expect in this day and age, extremely varied, both in method and in outcome. All of them represent a new simplicity that is already finding its architectural expression as we approach the turn of the millennium. It points the way towards a renewal which shuns the spectacular, values substance alone and, for that very reason, prompts confidence.

Vittorio Magnago Lampugnani is a professor at the ETH Zurich. He was the Chair for the 1998 and 2001 juries and the Director of the DAM when the exhibition *European Architecture 1984-1994* was presented there. This article was published in the catalogue.

Faith or Life: An Architecture Prize, Several Experts and the New Game of Vying for a Position

Dietmar Steiner

(1998)

The sixth Mies van der Rohe Award for European Architecture, the official architecture prize of the European Commission, was granted to the Kunsthaus Bregenz by Peter Zumthor. Austria is pleased with this result and, to a lesser extent, so is Switzerland. Austria is also pleased by the choice of the projects for the exhibition and catalogue, which included: the Faculty of Social and Economic Sciences at the Universität Innsbruck by Dieter Henke and Marta Schreieck, the Lower Austrian Regional Archive and Library in St. Polten by Michael Loudon, Karin Bily and Paul Katzberger, and the Department for Information Technology at the Technische Universität Graz by Florian Riegler and Roger Riewe.

The jury's decision in favour of Zumthor's art museum was made after an intensive basic discussion and only just ahead of that for the Villa in Bordeaux by OMA. In the course of this discussion, two very different positions in contemporary European architecture clashed within the jury represented by two extraordinary buildings. This was an all too prototypical illustration of the current state of the discourse.

So Rem Koolhaas's position is developed in the OMA's research laboratory and continued in a different form by the younger generation of Dutch architects. A dynamic, dialogue-based approach to architecture may be observed in the projects by Adriaan Geuze, MVRDV, Kas Oosterhuis, Lars Spuybroek, Willem Jan Neutelings and Michiel Riedijk and others. In contrast, Zumthor stands for an absolutist, autonomous architecture, a stance which is currently widespread in many other European countries.

The following considerations are afterthoughts to the discussion held by this jury. Positions that were discussed intensely twenty years ago are now re-emerging on the surface of the discourse. A new battle of ideological directions is spreading behind the postmodern entertainment/architecture's cult of stars. Both positions are admirably legitimate; it only remains for us to consider what will emerge from them. All contemporary forms of culture have their trends and fashions. But this is only apparently true. For if one looks at the facts of the situation more closely, then we see that this may be reduced to a media phenomenon or one of daily misinformation. Or there are concrete economic interests to be discerned underlying such trends as what we wear and the things we do every day.

Architecture is just as much a form of contemporary culture; however, the interests and positions represented are only indirectly determinable by comparable basic conditions. The reason for this is simple: there is no real 'market value' for architecture. The field of architecture has its 'stars', of course, but none of them by any means capitalise on their status in their projects in the way that painters or actors do. In other words, nobody can really become rich just from architecture. Today, architecture is a part of the culture industry; it is a marketing instrument. But one particular position of architecture is not physically linked to that.

In this way durable positions develop parallel to one another just as disparate ones do. Any one single valid position for the architectural future is, in any case, not determinable. One could even maintain that architects have emancipated themselves from the architecture where the stars are concerned. They are commissioned to fulfil expectations of a certain stance towards architecture, which means architecture with a signature and a predictable result. These are almost always first-rate achievements, but they do not really bear any kind of witness to broader cultural changes and developments.

Faced with this, each period has its mainstream. In the Europe of the 1990s architecture is determined, to put it succinctly, by two extremely contrary positions: a faction with an interest in technological purism on the one hand, demanding total autonomy for the art of building, and on the other a search for experimental strategies for dealing with the everyday. A little hindsight is needed in order to understand these contemporary positions. To put it very simply, one might say that the 1970s were a time of liberal social concern. This interest in the users of developments led to a search for an easily comprehensible architectural language in the 1980s. Postmodernism promised to provide this while at the same time being linked to propounding the autonomy of architecture. In the 1990s, however, it would appear that we have lost sight both of a sense of social responsibility and the search for the comprehensibility of the architectural language.

And the only thing remaining is insistence on the autonomy of architecture. This is understandable insofar as the inner-architectural system of references – the subculture of architecture – has grown enormously due to hype in the media. In other words, the 'community' of people purely interested in architecture – in the media, exhibitions, lectures, conferences, and so on – has become large enough today to allow architects and their positions to triumph in the collective consciousness.

This is one of the prerequisites for the communicative boycott of a purist minimalist 'sacred architecture'. This development in contemporary architecture is to be observed primarily in Switzerland, Spain, France and Austria, but also in Belgium, Germany and the United Kingdom. Minimalist architecture certainly has a variety of different origins and premises, but its common result is an abstract language of primary prismatic volumes. The issue addressed is the material process of the construction itself. The basic contrary position to minimalist architecture is currently to be found above all in The Netherlands. Starting there, the issue of a new, scientifically based architecture is presently being addressed, employing the technical means available today to arrive at a level of formal acceptance in the discourse. Here, architecture abandons its claim to autonomy and is starting to employ new concepts, strategies and signifiers in the attempt to enter into an exchange with the users and all the forces affecting the architecture.

Of course, the boundaries between these two positions (an autonomous architecture and one which is involved in a dialogue) are not fixed. In this way a dialogue-based premise can lead to a minimalist solution, while insistence on autonomy, on the other hand, can...what? Nothing, and that is the problem. Minimalist architecture insists on the typological and morphological consistency of the European town. It is a legitimate strategy of refutation as a cultural statement. The world of neoliberal deregulation, the world of staged events, the sensation, the dissipation and distraction: this world requires its counterpart, which may be the image of contemplation, of concentration, of the subtle difference, and the highest material demands. This is not a 'democratic' architecture, nor one capable of entering into a dialogue. And this form of architecture is perpetrated with an all too dictatorial absolutism.

In contrast to this, open dialogue-based architecture is always provisional and incomplete. It is involved in a process with the existing social forces. It does not represent an alternative to consumerism; instead the attempt is made to influence the forces behind it and to bring about a shift in these. This form of architecture is 'realistic' and open; minimalist autonomous masterpieces are also admired by its proponents as comprising a necessary position.

There is no doubt that dialogue-based architecture is more appropriate to our social situation than autonomous architecture. Nothing has changed here in these two positions since the debates of the 1970s. Today, dialogue-based architecture needs that respect which the autonomous position has earned, even for a silent architectural statement, to make its own position really tenable. But the diverse demands for a much-coveted claim to absolutism for autonomous architecture are finally also every bit as dubious as any other fundamentalist positions in social and political life. This debate also determined the discussion of the jury for this year's award. In this sense, the result is never objectively correct or incorrect, but it is always 'qualitatively democratic'. This means that an extensive and protracted process of selection with recommendations by experts, an illustrious jury in two sittings, and the concrete inspection of a final selection always eventually lead to a single winning project. This is the qualitative aspect of the result. The democratic aspect is based upon the unpredictable and erratic level of the experts' knowledge of European architecture, and on the individual profiles of the members of the jury within a process of group dynamics. This is why in the face of the qualitative highpoints of European architecture there can and shall never be one unanimously supported and infallible victor.

Dietmar Steiner has been the Director of the Architekturzentrum Wien AzW since it opened in 1993. He was a member of the jury from 1996 to 2001 and then again in 2007.

Architecture
IS
Propaganda

Elia Zenghelis

(2001)

The more bewildering the rate of change, the more amazing it is to notice how many things do not change and how much we count on them in our changing lives. Despite urban sprawl's claims to replace the city, the city is still there – a magnetic event – and *pace** Detroit, still teeming with its own seduction: 'The city is like a toilet', Andrea Branzi recently cried out to a shocked audience of scholars, 'you can build a bathroom as big as you want – it can grow to 1,000 square metres or more – but there is only one hot-spot.'[1]

In a firmament of instability, stable things mark time and space like beacons and none more so than the most intrinsically man-made edifice of all, the Arts. Our experiences of high art are confirmed in our ordinary culture and ordinary experience, and through this confirmation the ordinary is, to a certain extent, reformed and redeemed:[2] a synthetic remake, superior to the original, which we *often* miss. This is nowhere more eloquent in the telling and demonstration than in Proust's *À la Recherche du Temps Perdu*, where the evoked is superior to the real, the description superior to the event and the original experience uplifted: the superiority lies in the artefact, which distinguishes art from reality. It seems that our species has been engaged forever in its primordial obsession, manifested as a systematic build-up of our own, superior, *synthetic nature* as a substitute to the real – a drive to liberate ourselves from our bondage to the earthbound condition.[3] Architecture is a part of this enterprise and its emblematic rhetoric disconnects it from 'reality'.

The result is *pleasure*, and in the selection process for the Prize the experience of judging was in fact the experience of sorting out degrees of pleasure. In their evaluation, the polemics of the Jury were derived from *sensuous* experience. However, the substance of the argumentation soon took on an *ideological* complexion, which clearly demonstrated that despite the subjectivity of our response, architecture's authority is not personal but resides in the efficacy of an inner logic that possesses its own *dogmatic independence*.

To qualify these assertions, I should like to give a brief account of the Prize and the mechanics of the jury to set a frame of reference for this introduction. In this, I look at the background against which the present selection of work was made; I attempt to retrace some aspects of the inherited values in the years during which this work was carried out, a moment in time at critical crossroads; and – in the light of the high standard of works in this selection – I take this opportunity to ask some questions about where we are going and what we think of architecture.

What makes this Prize unique is that it is granted to a building rather than to a person, with the architect receiving the award on behalf of that building. As such, it is emphatically not a lifetime

Editor's note: * The use of latin 'pace' here means 'with the exception of'.
1. Andrea Branzi in a Venice University seminar on urban sprawl.
2. From a definition by Dave Hickey in *Air Guitar: Essays on Art & Democracy*. Democracy. Los Angeles: Art Issues Press, 1997.
3. Hannah Arendt's postulation in *The Human Condition*. Chicago: University of Chicago Press, 1958.

achievement award, disregarding as it does all forms of architectural contribution outside this definition. Presented at the Barcelona Pavilion (at once a paradigm and palimpsest), the search is for a European building whose level of achievement displays paradigmatic quality. Awarded biennially and restricted to work completed within the previous two years, the Prize's frequency also helps to level the playing field for all architects.

Nominations are made by experts in the participating countries who are not committed to designating buildings in their own country, but can propose up to five buildings within Europe. This year the number of entries had doubled, and since a remarkable proportion of these buildings were of high quality, selection was more than usually difficult. (And even so, jury members were surprised at the number of buildings they felt had been left out.)

Yet representing excellence in European architecture is not easy. The EU at the end of the century is in a position of development, midway between partial economic and political unity – with applicants waiting in the wings, while being compelled to respond to rebels who resist its appeal and pit themselves against its ideal for their own political, economic or hegemonic reasons. Hence, the figure of 'Europe' devolves into a changing pattern, which is hard to represent and from which it is harder still to elicit an emblematic culture, especially since talent 'bloweth where it listeth'. Some countries such as Switzerland and Andorra, among others (geographically within but politically outside the Union), find their architectural production excluded from consideration, even when its nationals build in EU countries. However, as buildings are part of the cultural heritage of the place in which they stand and the Prize is for a building, this created a paradox and a dilemma, which the jury was forced to overcome by maintaining that in certain instances, to paraphrase Gertrude Stein, buildings and places that were *there* were not there.

This jury procedure is democratic, operating on consensus. Its opposite, a award given by an individual, is *despotic* and arbitrary; however it can be *scrutinised* and given a retrospective explanation: its reason can be rationalised through its own criteria. The *democratic* decision has no explanation, it is *tautological*: its reason is that it is democratic. The jury, with all its passions and conflicts, is a microcosm of society; decisions are strenuously fought for and carried by debate in a time-honoured process of rhetorical supremacy, the fiery human art of persuasion which vindicates the decision.

By now it is only an historical curiosity to note that members of the jury making common cause today, could twenty years ago – even ten years ago – have been engaged in battle from opposite sides of a seemingly irreconcilable ideological chasm: sides disguised under banners such as 'Modernism' or 'Rationalism': a fight that left few untouched. No-one could foresee the present, in which these distinctions would be blurred into obscurity by an avalanche of architectural production, in which the formerly iconoclastic is recycled as commercial formula and the 'exciting' becomes distinctly suburban. With old modernist priorities exhausted – at least in their received form – today's jostling contenders seem only raucous claimants after an empty throne. Despite an exponential growth in architectural 'product' (and its supporting sunshine theory), we seem to have arrived – despite unprecedented loquacity and the endless tautology of the photoshop din – at a deafening silence, a strange void threatening to become an explosive vacuum. In this atmosphere of surfeit, and after ninety years of proselytising and lack of paradigm, we find a *breathing space*: a primitive hungering after 'essence', in which intrinsically *architectural* values emerge suddenly as our only guide.

As this Prize is set into the uncertain framework of the impending millennium (it is for the last two years of the century just gone), one cannot resist the temptation of a backward glance, because this century has been – for architecture – tyrannically puritan: full of adversity, contradictions, interrupted dreams; and at the century's demise, architecture is left captive to ideas to which it does not respond.

Modernism was the unprecedented feature of 20th-century art. However, the *social* dimension in its 'revolutionary' character gained a much more fundamental grip on architecture than on any of the other arts, producing a deep structural change to its practice and self-perception. Architecture was made subservient to social priorities with the assumed morality of 'function' tying it to programme and a dependence on *types*. By overlaying extraneous obligations onto it, *Modernism turned architecture from abstract to figurative* – the exact opposite of its impact on the arts. As abstraction was taking over 20th-century art, and indeed its civilisation, in architecture a code of morphological equivalences to programmes was codified into a typological iconography, a process seen as distinctly rational, in which it lost the rhetoric of its essential abstraction and, through this, its claim to beauty became taboo.

The iconography was justified, among other things, by the dictum that for the first time in history the masses had became the clients of architecture – if one can call people 'clients' who lack the power to command their preferences: a simple admission that exposes the gap between architecture's democratic pretensions and its authoritarian reality. In fact the urgency to house populations economically made architecture politically indispensable (and architects instruments of the State), in turn delivering it into the century's full spectrum of political ideologies. Ironically, whatever the political patron, social housing has emerged as everywhere the same; indeed, its standards have over time become capitalism's market normative, standards which even now are undergoing continuous refinement. This process reflects not architecture's triumph but our collusion: whether or not the housing industry becomes as streamlined as the car industry, the qualitative loss implied by '*existenzminimum*' has had a totalising impact on 20th-century architecture *beyond* housing and size, in which architecture has been forced to sneak into life, its 'recidivist' elements disguised or explained away. As foretold by the 1929 dissenters, a temporary compromise seems to have become a seemingly permanent self-castration, in which the Cavalier spirit of architecture has again been put to flight by a Roundheaded missing of the point.

Meanwhile, beauty has become the *poète maudit* of architecture: a word in bad odour, surreptitiously dropped from public debate, never featuring in the architectural discourse... Nobody dares mention beauty in public, even though in private it remains our ultimate measure of experience. Like shy virgins fearful of indecent exposure, we hold our innermost ardour – to be purveyors of beauty – as our most closely guarded secret; our sheepishness at being caught out has become our most ridiculous attribute since the Modern Movement began. This denial of beauty in the name of reason, precision or analytical expedience is evidence of a fundamental insecurity...

Beauty remains the rhetoric of how things look; as an iconography of change, it is a polemical instrument, vital to the evolution of architecture in its power to mark, represent and advocate the present, since it accounts for the vital ingredient of pleasure that we derive from it. Vital, not just in its conventional distinction from ugliness or pain but as that inclusive singularity in which beauty and ugliness, pleasure and pain are all together privileged as 'these extraordinary conditions over their true contrary: the banality of neutral comfort'.[4]

Meanwhile, function, typology and morphology acquired the momentum of a trinity which, in the course of the 20th century, turned the training of architects into a universal catechism, generating a series of rigidities that unfailingly became caricatures of the original ideological models. This has led architecture into a series of culs-de-sac from which it could not escape and where it has invariably met with humiliation, rejection and reaction from a recalcitrant public that persists in expecting more from its public art.

In this respect, the Barcelona Pavilion is a complete lesson in architecture: it is *palimpsest* in that its logic grows naturally out of the traces of what went before; it is *paradigm* in that its rhetoric broke with established conventions to become emblematic of modernity; and *iconoclastic* in that it refutes redundant overloads (in this case the overload of modernist 'moralism'), thereby restoring to architecture its innermost simple-minded logic: a confrontation between *itself* and activity in general. Its iconographic rhetoric is recognised by our experience, where it is automatically transformed and redeemed: we recognise it as a great work of art and a paradigm of *beauty*.

Theory, however, once established, becomes a *fata morgana*, always reappearing in circumstances of poor practice – and prolonging it. The 20th century has been a century of theories and their cumulative effect on architecture has been to castrate it. The inverse ratio between theory and architecture applies: architecture *is* its own theory. The CIAM congresses proved this fact by wrapping around architecture a formidable chastity belt (even as this was privately abused by some of the congress perpetrators who used their architecture as a liberating agent), and after World War II, more was enforced with a vengeance by Team X, CIAM's successors, who returned from the war possessed by the mercenary zeal of fundamentalist young Turks.

By the late 1950s, naked self-asserting architectures, now indecent, had been made dependent on a series of extraneous ideological layers, guarded in the name of integrity and social

4. Dave Hickey in *The Invisible Dragon: Four Essays on Beauty.* Los Angeles: Art Issues Press, 1993.

responsibility and mercilessly indoctrinated in schools. The fruits were disillusion and apprehension; the only relief was the enemy: the consumerist euphoria during the economic recovery of the 1960s. This was taken up by young and inspired rebels, Archigram being the most talented with prophetic visions, though ahead of their time and too amoral to fill the value-free (and explosive) vacuum of the decade – they were the harbingers of today's less visionary photoshop generation.

The *dénouement* of the 1968 explosion had the inverse to the desired effects: together with the institutional superstructure, it dismantled the ground below, generating a totalising absence of motive. Architecture had naturally failed to transform its nature to acquire political instrumentality, the anticipated *détournement* was not materialising on any plane and a state of aimlessness combined with the aftertaste of spent consumerism: conditions which had the effect of releasing an accumulated self-hatred among architects. Out of this desert, Superstudio's *Continuous Monument* and Archizoom's *No-Stop City* appeared with the limpidity of oases, wielding a revived, sheer and categorical architectural polemic with its iconographic rhetoric as their sole power.

It was at this moment that OMA was conceived: likening our situation with the shipwrecked raft of the Medusa, OMA set out to develop an architectural polemic to *preserve* and *reform* the modern project through projects that were critical and pragmatic; their purpose was to free Modernism from its puritanical shrink-wrap in the face of its complete ignominy. On the one hand, OMA saw architecture as territorial conquest and the plan as provocation of programmatic performance; on the other hand, it launched a polemic through projects against the 'new' historicist and typological architectures that were rapidly gaining ground, arguing that culture was at the mercy of a 'Procrustean' censorship against modern activities under the pretext that there is no room for them, while artificially reviving others that fit the *forms* and *types* they wished to resurrect. And it rejected the tyrannical superstition of architecture as problem solving, by emphatically demonstrating that there were no problems to solve.

With OMA's emphasis on *programme* as platform for social inspiration and mutable behaviour, the term *hybrid* was devised, though bearing a different meaning to the one currently in fashion: not a fusion of distinct entities into indistinct formal combinations, but an abstract framework for architecture, capable of absorbing an indeterminate number of activities (and on the principle that no *single* specific function can be *matched* with a single place), but stable enough to redeem the 'change that is life' and any form of destabilisation without affecting the framework itself.

Meanwhile, Spanish and Portuguese architecture, freed from the enforced hibernation and isolation of dictatorship (and inspired by early OMA), had by the early 1980s sprung forth with exemplary vigour, quickly reaching an astonishing degree of excellence, which has ever since led Europe in unmatched overall quality and quantity. While this is universally acknowledged and admired, for some (mysterious) reason it does not yet seem transportable and stays within the orbit of Iberian influence: it is curious how few architects outside this world seem capable of – or even interested in – drawing conclusions from its cultural polemic.

The apotheosis of 'polyvalent Postmodernism' in the 1980s had supplanted the uncontrolled and unjustified hatred of architecture with an uncontrolled and unjustified love – everybody loved it and, for once, the public too. Springing from dispersed corners of the earth, it became globalisation's arm, a spectacular success that reflected its value-free character and anticipated the so-called 'new' economy. With the crash of the late 1980s, it quietly withered away, leaving behind it a trail of architectural squandering of global proportions. By the early 1990s, with Postmodernism on the run, the love object was not there anymore.

In fact, this victory, this cleaning of the decks for a renewed and revived modern project, coincided with a period of unprecedented economic growth in an already prosperous Europe whose primary investments in infrastructure and housing were more or less complete.

But its prosperity was negligible compared to a new European discovery: striking gas and outmanoeuvring the lot, The Netherlands – Europe's (socialist) 'Kuwait', a state-projected media phenomenon and as yet unrumbled Trojan horse – has made in architecture an international hit with a spectacular display of extreme youth, controversial images, catchy slogans and iconoclastic claims that obscure the ineradicable conformity of the Dutch. It is as if an unprecedented government investment has generated a vast bureaucracy of iconoclasts. This paradox is to a large extent explained by Rem Koolhaas's cruel decision in the 1980s to make Rotterdam his headquarters, casting a shadow that is too big for the size of the country. Due to their mainly Protestant upbringing, the Dutch take him literally and whole, rationalising seemingly irreconcilable juxtapositions through reduction and in the process purifying this into a collective duty (even a tussle) to be iconoclastic. A subliminal resistance to humour – often perceived as unethical –, a total immunity to metaphors and an unwillingness to accept the existence of hidden meanings have together tended to generate misguided inspirations that result in stillbirths through bad cloning. Rem Koolhaas is too 'Mediterranean'– and it is striking that the few who are immune to this syndrome and retain their independent architecture come from the south, the 'Mediterranean' of The Netherlands.

Under these conditions, the resulting orgasm of Dutch construction becomes, in terms of mainstream European logic, truly 'iconoclastic'. In the space of a mere decade, the hard-won landscape of The Netherlands has been transformed by the spread of a vast network of low-rise, high-density business parks and (often stranded) suburbias, which altogether have set new groundbreaking *lows*, both in standards of construction quality and in the downward redefinition of maximum size for *existenzminimum*, whether public or private. The wonder is the lack of exposure and, given their earlier history of rebellion in the 1960s, apparent lack of self-criticism: it even seems like collusion.

The yes-no sequence that became the ebb and flow of architecture's fortunes since the 1960s has again gone full circle and we are experiencing the kind of unnerving restlessness that is typically generated under conditions of paradigmatic void. Once again architecture is being discredited by architects and again being deemed irrelevant and inadequate: this time to the prevailing directions of technological society – as if society *needs* architecture to pave the way. Its inability to rise to exotic claims (visualised in conjunction with the 'information highway') or to mutate society's programmes makes it the subject of derision. We have forgotten that architectural programmes stem *from* society, that architecture (which stems from civilisation) is part of the hardware that society needs. But that the two do not overlap or merge: this unlikely union is one of our chimeras and we are now optimistically engaged in making hardware behave like software. We have generated a non sequitur of rhetorical redundancy.

But it is important that we who conjecture can recognise and remove redundant overloads, which we will probably find in the intellectual and ideological overlays over architecture's modernism, rather than in the extraneous pressures impinging on it, i.e. economic, political, environmental, technological or any other enabling or disenabling agents.

There is a growing need for an iconoclastic clean-up operation; a transaction that will liberate architecture from phantom obligations. This can of course be achieved only through architecture; and only words of modesty can sustain this immodest craft: a simple-minded rhetoric by simple-minded orators (the likes of Leonidov, Le Corbusier, Mies or Kahn) whose idealism is limited to the corporeality of architecture and into which it transcends like vaccine. An architecture that has the efficiency to renew itself, 'generate its own successors'[5], evolve a polemic against phenomenal reality and transform the current relationship between architecture and programme into a confrontation between life and abstraction. Far from a revolution, this means an injection of young blood with the audacity to break with established convention and the kind of simple-minded idealism that immunises it from becoming the subject of the most terrible cloning.

Society is the primary infrastructure of the city; architecture requires (as hardware without catalytic effect) the stability to assimilate the unstable character of contemporary conditions in order to be efficient and able to host effortlessly and in silence the next course of events. Its new form of efficiency will be its rhetoric and will sustain the quality of present-day modernity: paradoxically it is the most elemental and orthodox means that are the most reliable resting-places of modernity.

In the end – and this is the sobering effect of awards for architecture – one must be reminded from time to time that architecture is about buildings, even though, as we know very well from history, they do not have to be built, or even be strictly buildable. Architecture *is* propaganda.

5. From "Architecture" in *Exodus* by OMA, 1972.

Elia Zenghelis has taught at numerous institutions such as the Kunstakademie in Düsseldorf and the Berlage Institute in Rotterdam. He was a member of the award jury from 1994-2001.

Monuments for the New Europe

Aaron Betsky

(2003)

As Europe falls and flails towards unity, it is shedding national constructions to the benefit of local flavours and mediated myths shot through with continent-wide legal codes and storms of images produced at an international level and raining down over every citizen.

The notion of architecture as a kernel of connection between physical reality and cultural representation is now becoming more and more important. The fundamental task of the architect is no longer to build homes for the central institutions of the State but rather to generate regional representations of larger organisations. An endless parade of schools, city halls, regional transit centres, community halls and sports facilities constitutes the bulk of what counts as significant architecture in Europe. Yet despite its diversity, much of this work shares a set of common characteristics. These include attempts to rescue a sense of realness, materiality or the image of specificity in the building; a fragmented, tortured and almost mute monumentality; a return to the basics of organisation and composition over an application of decoration or other extraneous elements; and a smart exuberance that reserves its resources for a few moments of great effect.

In other words, our most interesting current architecture is that which searches for a new way of making architecture in Europe. Far from claiming that there is one international or many national styles, it seeks to use the logic of construction, function and material to create identity. Such identity imbues its structures with a sense that there is a reason why they were built connected both to larger issues and structures, such as state bureaucracies, mass housing or transportation networks, and to the specificity of that building, that usage and that place. The results are difficult to classify beyond such generalities, although there are some things such architecture does not represent. It does not sink into the slippery application of skins without reference over standardised skeletons, as one sees in the buildings designed in Capitalist Modern along the roads to airports. It does not try to rescue a national style that was, in any case, usually invented in the 19th century. It is not closed, symmetrical and confident.

The works selected for the European Union Prize for Contemporary Architecture - Mies van der Rohe Award 2003 are all good buildings, but they are also something more and something less. In making the choice of forty-one buildings, much was omitted to single out this tenuous clarity, on both the aesthetic and functional levels: many private homes and many buildings with columns are not part of this selection. Thus, by its very selection of elements from various parts of this increasingly united continent, the choice represents the committee's role in attempting, as any pan-European group would do, to create a new myth, a new place and a new fact: the regional, rational, robust Europe.

Remarkably, though, this effort revolves largely around the act of stripping buildings down to their bare bones, either literally or in terms of their representational power. Abstraction, fragmentation and gestural deformation, which a decade ago were still part of the language of an avant-garde that had grown up under the sign of '68, have now become an integral part of the way the central institutions of local, national and continental power structures are designed.

Out of this effort of un-building previous certainties, a new set of concerns is entering the practice: how to address environmental issues within standard construction; how to preserve a sense of participation and democracy in a standardised situation; and how to create a sense of fun, verve or just difference in the monotony of the networked super-region of sprawl.

I would suggest that this groping towards a European architecture falls into at least four more or less distinct categories:

1. Flip It and Reverse It

The simplest approach through which European architects may establish a new realm for architecture is to use existing forms in unconventional ways. This occurs both at the level of such base elements of buildings as structure or materials and at the level of programme manipulation. Sometimes architects merely deform façades and plans to make something out of the banal, as Tony Fretton did with the Sainsbury House. In other cases, such as Commissariaat voor de Media by Koen van Velsen, the doubled M&M Houses by José Miguel Roldán and Mercè Berengué and the Imperial War Museum North by Daniel Libeskind, it is a question of fragmenting, cutting, stretching and otherwise deforming elements. This almost invariably has a symbolic purpose: in the case of the M&M or Sainsbury houses, to express the changed nature of the domestic sphere; in the case of the War Museum, to express the violence inherent to the building's programme.

Yet not all examples of this approach are so laden with import. Underlying the architects' working method seems to be the belief that what exists should be good enough: it is simply that we need to re-examine as well as re-use existing materials and typologies. In the case of buildings such as Sheila O'Donnell and John Tuomey's Furniture College or the Mortensrud Church by Jan Olav Jensen and Borre Skodvin, the effort is one of revealing the building materials as well as the rural prototypes to which these buildings respond within the spatial and constructional elements themselves. There is no overt message here, only the desire to make a building that allows us to see it clearly by stripping away the layers of style, imposed geometry or assumed coherence in both composition and antecedents that usually cloud our understanding of a piece of new construction.

The most radical project of this kind is the Hageneiland housing development by MVRDV. Here a standard row house is doubled on the lot, then cut apart and its constituent elements strewn around the site. The results are fragments of the row that remain recognisable as such, but also single homes that look like children's drawings of a house. This sense of getting back to basics is further enhanced by stripping the buildings of all extraneous elements and cladding them in one material only. And having thus got back to the basics with each individual house or set of houses, the architects then made a coherent and open living complex by cladding each of the pieces in a different material and composing the whole into a village of forms. The result is a real community, based on the most elemental parts of building, within the increasing sameness of sprawl that today covers more and more of Europe.

2. Modernism Fragmented: Towards Almost Nothing

If the designs in the first category seem to emerge from a desire to mine the new out of the old, those in the second do the reverse: they seek to find the most elemental parts of architecture by continuing in the direction of the always newer, more abstract, more technologically driven and more invisible. In some cases, this means showing that mass-produced materials can be used in careful, fragmentary ways as in the Palác Euro by DaM in Prague, where the building forms a condensation of the shapes around it and yet acts as a harbinger of a new world. In other cases, as in the Swiss Re Office Building by Bothe, Richter and Teherani, technology is used to make buildings less visible and more ecologically responsible. One might call this social democratic architecture and sometimes, as in the M-Preis Wenns Supermarket by Rainer Köberl and Astrid Tschapeller, it veers off into a witty and slightly nostalgic evocation of old dreams of the new.

In other cases, this is modernism at its most earnest. When Xaveer de Geyter sets his minimalist apartment blocks a-turning in the OMA plan for the Chassé district in Breda, he rescues the belief in endowing the modern urban landscape with abstract sculptural markers from the monotony into which such manipulation of generic elements had sunk. The pattern of glass and brick, behind which the diagonal steel bracing is visible, further fragments these monoliths, so that the whole dissolves into an interplay of planes. There is no meaning here, no history, and perhaps no future, only the sense that the here and now is ungraspable and vaguely exciting.

The most radical approach is the one adopted by Anne Lacaton and Jean-Philippe Vassal in their Palais de Tokyo. Technology here is not even the glass and steel of high-style modernism in which one might recognise an ideology, but rather the invisible wiring that makes this crumbling building usable. It is the calibration of exit paths, the strengthening of the structure and the redirection of flows within an existing construction. Architecture here is almost entirely invisible. And there *is* an ideology here, of course: the architects align themselves with those who say that the only way to remain critical in our controlled, reasoned society governed by aversion to risk is to operate under the radar, in stealth, through appropriation and misuse. Like the black-clad demonstrators at the economic summits, Lacaton & Vassal seek to make a statement through negation that dissolves into the walls of the existing city as soon as power structures try to tease it out into the open.

3. Back to the Land

If something remains of place in a unifying Europe, it is place itself. For some architects, discovering where one is at the simplest, most physical level is the beginning of the construction of an architecture that might be specific to the identity of one particular location, and by extension to that of the people who inhabit or use it. For Josef Pleskot, this location is the gardens of Prague Castle, for César Portela it is the coastline of Spain in the Fisterra Cemetery and for Florian Beigel it is the landscape of eastern Germany. In the latter case, architecture serves as a way to both recall and repair the landscape, as it does in the Track and Field Stadium in Olot by Aranda, Pigem and Vilalta.

The sad – or promising – fact, depending on one's perspective, is that sometimes the land does not have much to tell; it is entirely monotonous. And for this reason some architects also build their own sites. It may be an abstraction of the existing geography, as in Zaha Hadid's ski jump in Bergisel or in the Parc dels Colors by Benedetta Tagliabue and Enric Miralles, or else it may be a new space altogether, hewn out of the land to create a more perfect place that appears neither with the confidence of the modern nor with the fragmentation of the postmodern. Such new caves, like the Hedge House Art Gallery by Wiel Arets or the Eden Project by Nicholas Grimshaw, create separate worlds forming technologically or aesthetically near-perfect alternatives to the world above.

While such efforts might be the fruit of either environmental or purely aesthetic concerns, perhaps the most interesting pieces of architecture are those that mark the land in such a way that users are free to understand and re-use the environment. A sterling example of this is Marco Navarra's Strip Park between Caltagirone and Piazza Armerina. By painting the disused railroad tracks, piling stones up as steles and cleaning up the ruins of former stations, Navarra has created an architecture that connects to the land, to the past and to the existing communities of Sicily.

On a much grander scale, this is also what Zaha Hadid accomplished with her tram station outside Strasbourg, which won the 2003 Award. By marking out the open stretch of land into a parking lot, folding this plane up into a shelter for the tram and bus stop, and gesturing towards the suburban railroad line marking the edge of the site, Hadid managed to make a place out of a non-place. The building is almost invisible, rising up only into a single roof and a few sloping walls, but the impact of the skewed grid of lighting poles, of the marking for the car slots and of the re-alignment of the traffic patterns is immense. A new scale, a new material and a new aesthetic emerge almost invisibly out of this confused terrain. Hadid accepted the existing situation in this ex-urban node, then skewed, angled, flipped and formed it until she had created a new monument to and in sprawl.

4. Towards the New Monument
The act of making such a monument in and out of almost nothing denotes a new current emerging in European architecture: a very powerful current because it is also as old as the palaces, churches, castles and caves generated by the will to translate place into significant, three-dimensional structure. As Europe strips memory and myth away from nation and place, as a global economy and a global culture make everything more and more the same, more and more flexible and therefore more and more ephemeral, the desire to just build in and out of a place in a manner that can hold memory and therefore identity becomes stronger and stronger. This may not be an entirely positive development, however. In many cases, the desire to resist sameness is reactive and reactionary. It leads to the creation of bulwarks of assumed identity, clad in columns or native costumes that are exclusionary and false in their burial of modern technology, spatial relations and functions. The jury did not nominate any such projects. It did, however, turn to several buildings whose monumental qualities are charged with a sense of foreboding, loss and muteness. In some cases, these are literal memorials, such as the Soviet Special Camp Memorial Nr. 7 in Sachsenhausen by Till Schneider. In other cases, they are defensive bulwarks for religion (the Dresden Synagogue by Lorch, Hirsch, Wandel, Hoefer, Wandel and Wandel-Hoefer) or culture (the Vienna Museumsquartier by Ortner &

Ortner). Elsewhere, the architects have tried to monumentalise mundane programmes such as banking (the Granada General Savings Bank by Alberto Campo Baeza) or housing (Schots 1 and 2 by S333 Architects).

Yet a new kind of monument is appearing on the horizon. It is visible, for instance, in the Materials Testing Laboratory by Francesco Venezia, in the Multimedia Library by Dominique Perrault and in the Brugges Concert Hall by Paul Robbrecht and Hilde Daem. These buildings house institutions through which we as a society are trying to make sense of our world. They are temples of research and culture, where the legacy of the past provides the basis for experimentation. They bear the marks of fragmentation and flipping, of the desire to abstract in order to strengthen form, and of the moulding of geography into a new kind of coherence. They rise above such efforts in order to state, however romantically, the possibility of the sheer making of a communal thing in and out of a place.

The best example of this new monumentalism in this selection is Jürgen Mayer H.'s Scharnhauser Park Town Hall. It stands in the centre of a new town on the site of a former American army base on the outskirts of Stuttgart. The site could be anywhere in Europe, and yet it has a particular history. Mayer's design recalls the military colours that once dominated the site, as well as the site's brown fields and the architect's own memories of the tonalities of his youth. Out of such repressed sentiments and impressions a new structure arises that, though skewed and angled, is nonetheless massive and confident. It twists and turns itself out of the orthogonal grid in which it sits, releasing from its slipped roof a curtain of water that cascades around people as they enter and leave the building. This ephemeral peristyle introduces one to the design's big idea: the continual statement that subsequently undercuts the grandeur of civic structures. Inside, a stair hall in the tradition of countless such organising devices stretches up the building's entire height. Here the concrete walls, their smooth abstraction both forbidding and reassuring, angle away slightly, creating the sensation that all is not normally palpable. Around this disturbed place of circulation, the interior sign of the movement through sprawl in which all the citizens here partake, are the moments of respite, such as the art gallery, the council room and the library. These rooms are beautifully composed, but cut, sunk and elongated so that their certainty is never complete. And while bureaucrats manipulate the codes and rules, citizens meet and marry, and visitors marvel at the compact container that has given their humble ex-urban settlement such a grand place.

The jury for the 2003 Prize felt that the Scharnhauser Park Town Hall was excessively charged with overstatements and romantic bravura to deserve first prize, so instead they singled the architect out as the most promising young designer in Europe. I have no doubt that the desire to make buildings with such qualities of memory and aspirations to civic sense will lead this and other architects of his generation to design the masterpieces through which architecture will answer the call of representing what an identity mirrored, mapped and strengthened by place might look like in the coming European century.

Director of the Cincinnati Art Museum since 2006, Aaron Betsky is the former Director of the Nederlands Architectuurinstituut NAi, Rotterdam. He was a jury member in 2004 and 2005.

The Netherlands Embassy in Berlin OMA

Mohsen Mostafavi

(2005)

'The project carves the single structure implied by Berlin's regulations in two parts: a wall and cube. The carving continues inside the building, creating an erratic path from bottom to top, surrounded by regular office accommodation. The trajectory captures salient elements of Berlin's architecture outside the 19th century, Nazi, Communist.'

From *Content* by Rem Koolhaas

Koolhaas specialises in making the unexpected seem obvious, and the Dutch Embassy in Berlin is no exception to the rule. Building in a place where the concept of urban development is dominated by the notion of the city block as an opaque mass, he presumably felt compelled to subvert that model: blindly following the regulations was not an option. More significantly, however, the key to the success of the project is what he and his team at OMA achieve architecturally, spatially, urbanistically and programmatically. The solution deviates from the rules and yet works so well that it fits the site like a glove.

Precedent I

Many of Le Corbusier's projects, including early houses such as the Maison La Roche in Paris or the Villa Savoye at Poissy, or even later schemes such as the Carpenter Center in Cambridge, Massachusetts, constitute interesting parallels to Koolhaas's architecture. These projects are not so much visual models as inspirational catalysts, performative palimpsests. In Maison La Roche the vertical movement from space to space acts as a mechanism for unfolding the tiny house, cutting it open to the naked eye. It is also this unfolding which constructs the architecture. In a similar yet distinct manner at Poissy, you climb up through the house until you finally come to the roof and rediscover an open landscape where the view of the distant horizon is literally framed as if it were a picture, an artifice. At the Harvard University Carpenter Center, a ramp leads from the old campus towards what was supposed to become the future area of development, in the process cutting through the building: a public gesture both of passage and of viewing. It is debatable whether such gestures are always as interesting for the person who is doing the viewing from the outside as they are for those on the inside who are being watched. There are indeed some aspects of Jeremy Bentham's infamous Panopticon at play here, albeit on a more modest scale and without the connotations of discipline.

In his ground-breaking Kunsthal in Rotterdam, Koolhaas used a similar palette of operations such as the cut through the building or later, and more systematically, the idea of fusing ramp and floor in the manner of Parent and Virilio's oblique surfaces. But unlike a generation of contemporary architects whose references to the modernist tradition have tended towards the literal, Koolhaas's use of precedent has been elliptical and therefore more innovative. You can understand the connections with an earlier precedent, but you cannot see a one-to-one correspondence; and this from an architect who has sung the virtues of copying!

The Embassy

One of the key design elements of the new Embassy is the trajectory, the unfolding of the vertical circulation path through the building. The trajectory begins at the Embassy's entrance on Klosterstrasse, then carves its way through the main building site, creating an ascending external pathway before entering the cubic structure of the Embassy, where it passes along many of the usual daily functions of the building, as well as some unexpected ones, such as a fitness centre.

At times it puts the adjacent spaces on display, behind glass walls. At times it passes along the building edge, exposing the skyline of the city. In parts the floor is made of green glass, making you aware of the view below. Although the effect is slightly unnerving and voyeuristic, more importantly it gives you a sense of your position within a sectional three-dimensional scan of the building, the connection between the body and the building becoming completely denaturalised.

The effect of this experience is similarly registered on the outside of the building, where it also produces a sectional façade. The endpoint of the trajectory is a café and a meeting room at the top of the building. Here the ceiling mechanically slides open to reveal the sky. Throughout its journey the trajectory exposes the operations of the Embassy, a building type normally shrouded in secrecy. The idea that not everything need happen behind closed doors removes at least one of the veils of officialdom. At the same time it can be argued that the quality of the spaces – the shape and location of the offices, the presence of the café, the views – has a direct effect on the way people work within the building. These material conditions construct a particular mood which in turn comes to stand for the great Dutch tradition of humanism. The Dutch, with their mercantile and pragmatic heritage, are clever enough to know that this is not a bad message to convey to the outside world. In fact, it is hard to imagine any other nation that would be prepared to resist the often justifiable paranoia about security by making such a metaphorically and physically transparent building. It is also from this contemporary Dutch perspective that the trajectory views the city of Berlin and its memories.

'The beauty of Berlin, its opacity, complexity, its heaviness, the richness of its ghosts. The abundance of good intentions that somehow went wrong. The pressure of shame imposed by more and more monuments. The obligation to remember, combined with the surprising amnesia (where did the wall go?). How far it is removed from everything. How refreshingly German it remains. Its greyness. Its stubbornness. Its lack of doubt. The meticulous mediocrity of its new substance. How old what was modern looks. How fresh what is ancient. How good what was Communist. How Chinese what is new.'

From *Content* by Rem Koolhaas

For Koolhaas the Dutch Embassy building is also a radical critique of the kind of false history that has been the intellectual armour of a core group of architects in Berlin. Clearly the conceptual project of a physically continuous urban fabric is disrupted by the fact that the building stands on a raised glass base and does not fill the whole site. But it is the very dissonance of the various elements of the building that produces its dynamic urban presence. Besides a small park along the River Spree, these elements include the wall building of the Embassy staff residences. The structure is in part a buffer set against the adjacent buildings and in part a perforated metal screen. The apartment of the Deputy Ambassador is accessed along a long corridor. Its living room is double aspect, but on the side facing the Spree the view is partially interrupted by the cantilevered sky-box that protrudes from the same floor in the Embassy where the Ambassador and his Deputy have their offices. This sky-box is the place for special meetings, a viewing room suspended in mid air. The amalgam of this inhabited wall with the carved open space of the trajectory on the outside, the cube of the Embassy building, and the park together make up the totality of the project.

The juxtaposition and the careful placement of these fragments create an overall coherence that is nevertheless subject to constant change, in terms of the relationships of spaces as well as the resulting views. These relationships are further enhanced by the choice and the proximity of different materials – glass, perforated metal, mirror, steel, wood, stone – and by the textures and colours of surfaces. The overall effect is one of lightness, of airiness, giving the building a fundamentally anti-monumental character. It is a quality that is almost ornamental in the richness and tonality of its palette.

Precedent II
Since the time of the International Building Exhibition (IBA) in the 1980s, Berlin has been the subject of numerous discussions regarding its role as a European city and the means by which it should recuperate the destruction inflicted on it not just by World War II but by modern architecture, and more specifically by the large residential projects of the 1950s and 60s. Against this background some Berlin architects have come to argue, often with justification, against modern architecture's capacity for urban reconstruction (they include Hans Kollhoff, who ironically shares with Koolhaas the intellectual experience of having studied with O.M. Ungers at Cornell). The policy of the city has been to achieve urban reconstruction by connecting the new development with the historical core of the city, in the process creating as much continuity and homogeneity as possible.

In this context the historical city, as the original source of reference, has come to dominate the discussion among both politicians and architects. The outcome has been a more singular architecture. Again one of the key (and in fact legitimate) arguments of this conservative position has been to support and promote the notion of anonymous architecture as the core material artefact of the city. But in reality, architects like Kollhoff are not anonymous architects and they certainly do not want to produce anonymous architecture. What they end up doing, perhaps inadvertently, is giving anonymity a dominance that it never had in the historical city. Anonymous architecture was and still is the backdrop for the daily events of the city but it has now moved into the foreground of visibility. A new form of monumentality is masquerading as the anonymous and the everyday.

This position bears a resemblance to the critique of the Modern Movement after World War II and the search for a new monumentality that would overcome the limitations of the private residential architecture of the Modern Movement. In Berlin, however, the new monumentality of the city's reconstruction projects is too burdened by the fact that it emphasises the representational qualities of public architecture rather than the creation of a setting for public engagement. That is why the transformative, dynamic and temporal qualities of OMA's Embassy building suggest a more productive understanding of precedent as a tool for the imagination, as well as optimism about the possibilities of a genuinely modern, projective, and forward-looking architecture of the city. It was in recognition of these achievements that we, the members of the jury, chose the Embassy as winner of the 2005 Prize.

Mohsen Mostafavi is the Dean of the Harvard Graduate School of Design and the Alexander and Victoria Wiley Professor of Design. He was a jury member for the 2005 award and he chaired the jury in 2011.

REWARDING EXCELLENCE

RICKY BURDETT

(2007)

The European Union Prize for Contemporary Architecture - Mies van der Rohe Award is an intense journey for its jury members; made all the more intense this year by the fact that 2007 constitutes the 10th anniversary of what has grown to become Europe's most distinguished architectural prize since it was first launched in 1987. Following in the footsteps of previous winners – Norman Foster, Álvaro Siza, Rafael Moneo, Dominique Perrault, Zaha Hadid, OMA/ Rem Koolhaas, Ellen van Loon, Nicholas Grimshaw, Esteve Bonell and Francesc Rius, and Peter Zumthor – is not an easy task, but the jury was convinced that the decision to award the 2007 Prize to Mansilla & Tuñón for the MUSAC cultural centre in the Spanish city of León will be seen as a confident statement in the future of European architecture in the first decade of the 21st century. Mansilla & Tuñón will certainly look back at this as a defining moment in their careers, as will Bevk & Perović, recipients of the Emerging Architect Special Mention.

As chairman of the jury, I have presided over a long and painstaking process of selection, a bottom-up process which considers nominations from architectural and professional institutions across Europe. 272 projects were presented to the jury in the form of a well laid-out exhibition in Barcelona – a rare and privileged cross-section of what is being produced in Europe at this very moment in time. To reach our conclusion, we had arguments and debates to narrow the list down to the forty projects included in the 2007 shortlist, illustrated in the catalogue and accompanying exhibition.

We had a much more difficult time to reduce the list down even further for the finalist shortlist. I think this level of tension and debate was a good sign. We wanted to have a maximum of four projects which we could visit over two days within a relaxed time frame. But we realised that we could not simply trust the images and photographs presented to us when it came to which projects we should leave out. Individual jury members were keen to understand how some intriguing projects worked in terms of satisfying their briefs as dance centres, museums, cultural centres or universities, and how they succeeded or failed to integrate with their differing urban contexts. So, after prolonged discussion we embarked on the logistical nightmare of visiting seven buildings over three days in the middle of April 2007. To the credit of the Mies van der Rohe Foundation team, everything worked out perfectly.

It is important to reiterate the importance of visiting the buildings 'in the flesh' when it comes to reaching a decision on the Prize. This particular jury seemed to be clear that the final winner should not simply be a building of great architectural quality, but that it should speak to its context and satisfy its programme. We therefore travelled to and looked intensely at seven buildings zig-zagging across Europe from the Mediterranean to the Atlantic, from Spain to Portugal, and through France to Germany.

In Valencia we visited David Chipperfield's generous America's Cup Building at the heart of a regenerating port area. In Portugal we travelled to the coastal town of Sines to experience the subtle shapes of Aires Mateus's Centre for the Arts. In Wolfsburg we saw the voluptuous volumes of Zaha Hadid's Phaeno Science Centre after visiting UNStudio's sculpted Mercedes Benz Museum in Stuttgart. In France we enjoyed the volumetric power of Rudy Ricciotti's Dance Centre in Aix-en-Provence and the well-mannered rigour of the School of Management by Lacaton and Vassal in Bordeaux. But it was the economy and intensity of Mansilla & Tuñón's MUSAC art gallery in León that grew on individual members of the jury as we moved from city to city, from building to building.

For the jury, MUSAC succeeded at three levels: architectural, urban and programmatic. Firstly, the architecture of MUSAC employs an exceptional economy of means to great poetic effect. The jury was impressed by the sense of delight and joy as one walked in through the front door of the art gallery. We had all studied the drawings and seen the photographs but the proportion, sequence and materiality of the spaces added up to more than the sum of their parts, creating a powerful sense of efficiency and optimism that transcends the conventions of architectural language. Secondly, the building seemed to work with the city in ways which, I must confess, were unexpected. Located in a soulless suburban area of this great cathedral city of León, it successfully embraces the urban context by creating a public space that is well used by younger people at different times of the day and evening, celebrating its fundamental civic and social function. Thirdly, MUSAC demonstrated a unique ability to fit its original programme as an open and experimental art gallery. Like a well-worn glove, the building feels comfortable for the art it carries. Whether it was video art or a conventional three-dimensional exhibition or a provocative sound installation, each oeuvre felt at home in this new building. As such it revealed a perfect fit between architecture and programme, between architect and client.

For these three reasons MUSAC received the 2007 Prize. It is important that these motivations are not only understood within the design professions but that they are shared by client bodies, both public and private, and government authorities. Without good clients who are ready to take risks and invest in good design, the future of architecture in Europe is under threat. Only by recognising that great architecture has a profoundly social, urban and aesthetic function – as the Prize does – can we look forward to at least twenty more years of buildings of lasting excellence in Europe.

Ricky Burdett is professor of urban studies at the London School of Economics and Political Science LSE and Director of LSE Cities and the Urban Age programme. He was the Chair of the jury for the 2007 award.

Luis M. Mansilla & Emilio Tuñón

In Conversation with Luis Fernández-Galiano

(2007)

Barcelona, May 14, 2007

Luis M. Mansilla_ A lot of what happens in life is a mixture between volition and chance. My father was a naval engineer, while on my mother's side there were links with art. The time came to choose a career so I asked my twin brother, 'What do you want to be?' 'A naval engineer', he replied. 'Well, I'm going in for architecture'. Just to be different. It sounds a bit ridiculous but that's the way it was.

Emilio Tuñón_ There's a curious parallel: my father was a seaman and my brother was a naval engineer too. It was my intention to be a naval engineer, but seeing my artistic gifts my mother encouraged me to be an architect. Thanks to that, I discovered a beautiful new world.

LM_ We were fortunate enough to be able to study at the Madrid School of Architecture (Escuela Técnica Superior de Arquitectura de Madrid), and we often think about the earnestness and professionalism of the teachers there, but above all about the way they managed to transmit their passion for the discipline.

ET_ I remember that Juan Navarro Baldeweg opened a door which leads you into a world you'll never leave again. Like Rafael Moneo said in one of his lectures, you come to see everything through architecture, and that's something which stays with you for life. And above Navarro and Moneo stood the figure of Sáenz de Oiza, the grand master of the Madrid School whom we all admired.

LM_ I believe that training was decisive, and it reached an even higher degree of complexity when subsequently we worked at Rafael Moneo's studio. As everyone knows, it's a very disciplinary studio, which lays great emphasis on meticulous analysis of reality and on the endeavour to solve the technical – not just the artistic or cultural – problems of architecture. This gave us a very solid grounding to set off on our own. Really, we couldn't possibly understand our work without having gone through those ten years of effort and discipline at Rafael's studio. We were involved with the Pilar and Joan Miró Foundation in Mallorca; I worked on the project for the Thyssen-Bornemisza Museum from beginning to end; and we entered in for lots of competitions at that time. It was a fascinating experience because we learned that architecture consists of many layers, and you have to make these layers coincide. What I mean is you might be making an almost intellectual reflection on architecture and at the same time reflecting on the client, on the programme, on the site, and you have to combine all this. I think we learned a fine lesson that's proved very useful to us ever since.

ET_ The Atocha Station was the project in which I personally worked closest with Rafael and a lot of effort was involved in collaborating with engineers. Everything was very complex. Eventually, in 1992, which is when Rafael came back from Harvard and all the '92 celebrations had come to an end, Atocha was inaugurated… We decided that the time had come, after ten years, to assume responsibility for our own work, so we came to an agreement with Rafael and set up our own studio.

229

The First Works: Zamora, León and Castellón

LM_ First Zamora, then the León Auditorium and finally the Castellón Museum represented a way for us to lay our cards on the table. We didn't know how to play, but that's when we laid our cards out. The Zamora Museum took almost three years to build and the project had taken us another three to prepare; at that time we did practically nothing else. Both as we were drawing up the project and while it was being executed, we reflected deeply about the combination in architecture of equality and diversity. It's a very simple idea, but we regard it as important in relation to society and we intend to develop it as a permanent feature of our work. It was then also that we began to look on the context as something non-formal, which was the main debate at the time: about how the relationship with the site may become something very abstract; abstract in a certain sense and yet very material, because we always wanted to bring these two extremes together. And finally we reflected on recognition of public space as something truly important when it comes to defining buildings. Those three cards were laid out then, and we're still playing with the same ones. We shuffle, deal and the game starts again, above all in the form of competitions, which not only have a democratic aspect that fascinates us but also constitute a permanent training that prevents us from becoming like hermits when we research. We enter ten competitions a year and each month we ask society whether what interests us also interests them.

ET_ We understand architecture as resting on three pillars: intellectual, educational and critical. It seems you have to reflect on the world and analyse it, and in terms of this vocation we gained certain experience by contributing to the architecture journal published by the Professional Association of Architects. And when that phase came to an end, we decided to create a small fanzine, *Circo*, a bulletin we sent to our friends, not so much with the idea of publishing a journal in the strict sense but rather of exchanging ideas with friends. We called it a 'thought cooperative', similar to the Expressionists' 'Crystal Chain'. This was complemented by the school, where we started giving classes in 1986, while we were still working in Rafael Moneo's studio. Eventually it occurred to us that *Circo* and our teaching activities needed to be rounded off by critical activity, which took the form of compilation of the classes we gave.

LM_ Our teaching activities subsequently extended to other universities, beginning in Frankfurt, when Enric Miralles sent for us. That was a wonderful experience we recall with great affection. Then we were at the school in Lausanne, last year in Harvard, another fascinating experience we're very happy about, and next year we'll be in Princeton. But we always keep a year free in between to devote ourselves to the studio.

Geometry, Colour and Context in the MUSAC

LM_ The city with which we've had the longest relationship is undoubtedly León, first with the auditorium and now with the MUSAC. I believe we've spent eight years of our lives travelling there practically every Thursday. It was a highly attractive opportunity to construct two buildings close to each other in a city, which also explains to a certain extent that relationship we spoke about between equality and diversity. Here we play with restriction – which I'd say is another card that's suddenly appeared in our pack –, in which making reference to the city's Roman origins we use Roman paving in the form of squares and rhomboids, endeavouring with this system to achieve maximum variety in a context of extreme rigidity. I think this is the most attractive aspect: what appears a little more on the façade or more obviously in the León Auditorium in a way disappears in the MUSAC, because in fact you might say that the form is no longer of any interest. There's that intellectual concern with reflecting on the form of things as something coming from outside, although there is a set of very material references to the city. Through the paving we refer to the agricultural landscape, something that has always fascinated us, those ploughed fields arranged according to a rigid inner order but with vague perimeters. There's a reflection on architecture as a mathematical field, that is, as the sum of parts that makes no reference to origins. I think we were incredibly lucky when we were given this difficult brief: they told us we were going to create a very big building with only a ground floor. That gave us a lot of food for thought about how mechanisms we'd traditionally defended in section could now be applied to a ground floor.

ET_ Actually, the project was based on that flexible, versatile organisation provided by geometrical meshes and mathematical fields, until one day the managers turned up demanding the presence of video walls on the entire façade. The price of video walls is so astronomical that they would have cost five or six times the building itself, so the idea was scrapped. But they asked us to put some colour there just in case, as if video walls might be added in the future. During the construction process, those managers disappeared and new ones came onto the scene. So we said 'Well, perhaps we might make the whole building more neutral'. And it was wonderful when the client said 'Hey, you promised us colours and we want colours!' It was then that we decided, after a long thought process, to choose the colours as if they had nothing to do with our own personal decision. It became a question not of choosing the colours but rather of extracting them from León's great public monument, the cathedral, whose interior is full of colours, turning it inside out and transforming it into an exterior using the colours of León cathedral's oldest stained glass window, the Falconer's Window. Then we digitalised it, pixelised it and placed it on the façade with colours that while they don't allow you to recognise the figuration, are nonetheless so potent that they are intelligible.

A professor at the Escuela Técnica Superior de Arquitectura de Madrid, Luis Fernández-Galiano is the editor of *AV Monografías* and *Arquitectura Viva*. He was a jury member for the 2007 award when the MUSAC by Luis M. Mansilla (1959-2012) and Emilio Tuñón received the Prize. Published here are excerpts of his conversation with the architects on May 14, 2007.

New Members: New Voices

Peter Cachola Schmal

(2007)

The jury of the 2007 European Union Prize for Contemporary Architecture - Mies van der Rohe Award was very happy to choose a new voice from Slovenia for the Emerging Architect Special Mention. With great self-assurance, Matija Bevk (born 1972) and Vasa J. Perović (born 1965) presented an impressive body of work to the jury. Projects by Bevk Perović Arhitekti had already been nominated for the past two editions of the Mies Award, in 2003 and 2005 respectively, and the young office has won the most prestigious national prize in Slovenia, the Plečnik Award for Architecture, three times in only the last four years. As a partnership, therefore, they are not entirely unknown.

Bevk started collaborating loosely with Perović in 1997 when nearing the end of his studies in Ljubljana, where he graduated in 1999. Perović is not even of Slovenian origin, but was born in Belgrade, Serbia, where he received his Diploma in Architecture in 1992. He went on as a postgraduate to complete a Masters in 1994 under Herman Herzberger and Kenneth Frampton at the Berlage Institute in Amsterdam. The cosy, family-like atmosphere there helped him a lot in terms of international networking.

An astonishing total of three projects built by Bevk Perović Arhitekti in 2005 and 2006 were nominated for this year's Award, all of them located in Ljubljana. The Polje Social Housing, with seventy-eight units, is a lesson in how materials and colour can be used to unify a scheme. The Student Housing, with fifty-six units, is a superbly crafted and elegantly executed ensemble, which addresses issues of public versus private spaces and explores their architectural treatment. A handful of private residences and several housing projects sum up the professional experience of this young practice. This second project would therefore have been perfect to represent their approach. Nevertheless, the jury chose the third project, the Faculty of Mathematics at Ljubljana University, for the Emerging Architect Special Mention.

This new building, so the jury said, 'is not a building in the standard sense of the word. It is, in fact, an addition, a three-storey slab built on top of the existing two-storey building.' The plan dates back to a 1961 project for two new university institutes, of which only one was completed at the time, while the other one was simply left at a reduced height of two storeys. In 1999, the young architects were asked to propose a solution on how to complete the original concept. The existing building could easily accommodate additional loads, as these had originally been factored in; however, there was a major access problem, since the existing building had already been sold to a private owner.

Bevk and Perović suggested using the roof of the existing structure as the new building site, like an oversized pedestal. It is this bold conceptual move and the subsequent clarity and consequence with which the concept was realised that so appealed to the jury.

This is a radical and extreme approach to 'sustainability' in architecture: instead of tearing down an inefficient building, it is instead simply used as an artificial basement for a new structure that occupies its air rights.

The design concept treats the new three-storey volume as a solid building mass from which a series of transparent, hollow spaces are carved out to show its public use. An elegant glass skin, screen-printed with different densities of a bar-code pattern, serves both to provide shade and as a visual system defining programmatic differences. Only the communal sections, such as foyers and waiting areas, boast clear transparent glass façades, thus fostering a visual dialogue between the interior and the urban context. It is a stunning sight especially at night time. In terms of circulation, only a small part of the ground floor plan is occupied by stairs and elevators, while the actual foyer spreads out on the second upper level, the new ground floor of the Faculty of Mathematics. An additional fire escape has been added on the side, while the lower building is oriented towards the back with its separate entrance there.

The budget for this project was extremely tight, but the architects managed with a simple, nonchalant and charming approach. The high-quality detailing and execution is rooted in a highly sophisticated local crafts tradition, kept alive even during the socialist Yugoslav era. The link to the neighbouring Faculty of Physics was solved in an equally straightforward way by planting a few trees in the existing asphalt parking lot and protecting the newly-defined central footpath from parked cars with a long concrete sitting bench and a row of bicycle stands. Simple, yet strongly voiced – this symbolic intervention works.

What Matija Bevk and Vasa J. Perović have accomplished is the essence of that which defines excellence in architecture, and thus stands at the heart of the Prize: they have created a building that offers more than functional and programmatic fulfilment and outstanding aesthetic qualities, while at the same time contributing to the urban fabric. They have erected an excellent place to live and work for their anonymous and future users, thereby fulfilling the social objective of building a new and inspiring world. And that is why the jury welcomes them into the honourable circle of the ten Prize and four Special Mention laureates to date.

We hope that this Award helps to direct more attention to this small Adriatic country with its population of only two million people and new member of the European Union and the Eurozone, which they joined in January 2007. Andrej Hrausky from the DESSA Architectural Centre attributes the hybrid nature of his country's architectural culture to its location: 'The geographical position on the very edge of the Slavic world, squeezed between Austria and Italy, gives us the opportunity to understand both the precision of the German world and the Mediterranean flair of Romance culture.'

Indeed, in Slovenia a rich architectural past and a promising contemporary architectural scene awaits us. For example, Slovenia has contributed to the world of architecture the outstanding genius of Jože Plečnik (1872-1957), who was rediscovered in the late 1980s as an individualistic artist who addressed issues of regionalism, collaging and sampling in architecture well before Postmodernism had even been invented. Still widely unknown, Slovenian architect Edvard Ravnikar (1907-1993) certainly bears rediscovering. He continued the work of his two teachers, Plečnik and Le Corbusier, in a very sculptural and expressive manner, and built extensively in the 1960s and 70s. His *magnum opus* is a complex of two eccentric towers with a conference centre built in 1972 on the Republic Square in Ljubljana, which now house the largest Slovenian bank.

The huge socialist planning collectives in Slovenia collapsed in the 1990s, as they could not cope with the requirements of free trade and competition that the new era brought with them. A young generation of architects grasped their historical chance, having been educated partly in other countries and having kept in close contact with their international counterparts. This very interesting scene includes not only the well-known Sadar Vuga practice, but also such teams as Dekleva Gregoric, Elastik, Maechtig Vrhunc, Monochrome, Ofis and Enota – whose hotel in Podcetrtek was chosen as part of the forty shortlisted projects for the 2007 Prize. Some of them were presented in the *Sixpack* exhibition that toured widely in recent years. Their task is nothing less than to reinvent Slovenian architecture at an optimistic moment in time.

Peter Cachola Schmal is the Director at the Deutsches Architekturmuseum DAM in Frankfurt since 2006. He was on the jury of the 2007 Prize.

The Age
of the
New Platforms
Francis Rambert
(2009)

What if excellence in architecture were to take an urban form? By this I mean putting the city first; likewise the relational aspect of projects, the hybrid content of buildings... The five finalists for the 2009 European Union Prize for Contemporary Architecture - Mies van der Rohe Award were selected on the basis of this essentially urban order, which sees functionality as indispensable, though secondary.

What role have they sought in the city? Where do they fit in? The response to such questions by these often ground-breaking projects confirms a trend: that of opening up new urban possibilities.

The Prize had already identified this trend in 2003, when it chose Zaha Hadid's Hoenheim-Nord Terminus and Car Park in Strasbourg, and in 2005 with Rem Koolhaas and Ellen van Loon's Dutch Embassy in Berlin. These two buildings, so different in écriture, programme and function (one wholly concerned with mobility, the other with representation), illustrate this fundamentally urban strategy. We recall, for example, how in the reunified German capital OMA did its utmost to invite the city into the building by establishing continuity through a singular 'pathway' that runs through the heart of this complex structure.

The 2009 shortlist contains further examples of this approach, based on connection and continuity. Apart from the obvious disparity in budgets, the urban contexts are also very different: a prestigious university in the heart of Milan; a local library in Barcelona; a Zenith music hall on the outskirts of Strasbourg; a tramway terminal in the suburbs of Nice; and an opera house, emblem of the conquest of an Oslo fjord. All are distinctive, and all firmly reject the 'generic city' model, which would produce globalised architecture or even no architecture at all.

With its angular stance, the Luigi Bocconi University, a magnificent work designed by Grafton, responds not without a certain austerity to the serious context of the Italian economic capital. A fortress in appearance, it asserts its openness by affirming its urban nature and its harmony with the neighbourhood.

By using the whole depth of a block, the Sant Antoni Library in Barcelona, RCR's project to rehabilitate a former industrial site, carves out a new urban space. Visitors pass through the great metal gate to discover how closely the architects have stuck to the existing development in creating this public place. Highly porous both visually and physically, the project sets up a close relationship with its surroundings.

Taking advantage of a suburban strip alongside the motorway, the Strasbourg Zenith stands out for its extraordinary aesthetic appeal. Draped in its mesh skin, the icon formed by Massimiliano and Doriana Fuksas's orange 'coliseum' may look like one of the circuses that pitch their big tops on the edge of town, but it fulfils its role as a large-scale venue to perfection. Visually, its play of ellipses starts the spectacle, which after nightfall is continued by the architecture itself.

By reversing a dead-end situation, Marc Barani's work on the tramway terminal slotted so intelligently into a plot at the southern end of the heights of Nice proves to be as concerned with mobility as it is with topography. Here is an example of how infrastructure can intentionally change its status, becoming pure architecture. Fitting into the scheme of things without losing contact with the sea: this is the performance here.

By deliberately opening the Oslo Opera House to the city, SNØHETTA also succeeds in bringing to life a neglected area cut off from the rest of the capital by a motorway. As well as a well-resolved reconquest of the site that inspired the transformation of the whole area, this work must be seen as the metamorphosis of a monument into an eminently urban space. More than an opera house, this building is first and foremost a public space.

Looking back to the harbour station built by FOA in 2001 in Yokohama, Japan, much more a public space open to all rather than just a travel terminal, we can see this same radical posture. Still earlier, in 1995, it was another Prize winner, the National Library of France in Paris, which ushered in this generation of buildings as public spaces. Dominique Perrault's monument-platform is a pioneer in this respect.

The Oslo Opera House falls squarely within this new urban 'version' of city practice. You need not be an opera lover to make use of the building, or a music lover to appreciate this architectural symphony 'in public space major'. The Opera House emerges from the cold waters to connect the city more closely to the sea, and the public can appreciate this quality both inside and out. The building sets the visitor in motion in a new test of the *fonction oblique*, a theory originally developed by Claude Parent and Paul Virilio. The 'fifth facade' of its roof is brought fully to life. Unlike the Sydney Opera House, the building sacrifices its status as monument by introducing a new dynamic to devote itself to and join forces with the city. An immersion in the urban universe perfectly portrayed in the photographs of its inauguration, which show the crowds engulfing the building.

The Oslo Opera House revives the culture of public space so marvellously exemplified by mythical buildings like Piano & Rogers's Pompidou Centre in Paris and Lina Bo Bardi's Museum of Art in São Paulo. The National Library of France in Paris, the Guggenheim in Bilbao, the Tate Modern in London, the Oslo Opera House, are all cultural spaces that are increasingly becoming the new driving forces behind urban development. But the Opera

House by SNØHETTA aspires to be more than a monument, to the point of rejecting the iconic status that today's world so delights in. It puts the monument in motion; it escapes from the static by crossing logics and flows. Creating its own topography, it embodies the continuity of urban space. And in doing so, it militates against the many kinds of breakdown that create so much of our wasteland.

The challenge today is to create new urban landscapes, bring forth new typologies of place. And why not, to replace the word 'place' by the term 'urban amenity'. This is how these new platforms, these urban catalysts, appear. The fact that the final debate of the jury was focused on two building-platforms (the Oslo Opera House and the Nice Tramway Terminal), so dedicated to the city, is a telling sign.

Indeed, over and above its reward in prestige terms, the Prize has another significance. It both indicates the state of health of European architecture and acts as a seismograph of activity in the debate on the contemporary city. At a time when metropolises worldwide are searching for their place in the new post-Kyoto order, the Oslo Opera House sends out a clear message: urban space offers real ground for experiment.

Francis Rambert is the Director of the Institut français d'architecture Ifa, Cité de l'architecture & du patrimoine since 2003. He was a jury member for the 2005 and 2007 award editions and he chaired the jury in 2009.

What is Quality Today?

Ole Bouman

(2009)

Let us be frank: the biennial European Union Prize for Contemporary Architecture - Mies van der Rohe Award for the best European building is currently facing a dilemma. It either has to stick to its definition of quality, or adjust that definition in order to maintain its position as the key indicator of architectural excellence on the continent. It either defends its cultural legitimacy to honour a marvellous building as a building, or it adapts to the dynamics of building itself: the shift from object to performance, from shape to programme, from visual to social effect, from physical fact to convincing story. A painful dilemma, to be sure, because the price to pay for either option will be high.

This antithesis is more than a frivolous theoretical exercise or a regression to ideological battles of the past. It reflects one of the fundamental problems of architecture today: where does its cultural relevance reside? Actually, this is not really a contemporary issue. It is a timeless question that usually seems to be restricted to a small group of rare personalities for whom it is not enough just to practise architecture as a matter-of-fact business: they want to know the reason behind it. Most of the time it is the prerogative (and predicament!) of people who are born with a reflexive inclination. Normally they stay out of the spotlights.

Not this time. This eternal search for purpose has now acquired the aura of existential necessity. It is no longer a harmless issue; it is a question the answer to which may possibly decide the fate of the discipline. We had better realise sooner rather than later how existential it is.

'Come on, aren't you exaggerating a bit?', the reader might ask. Perhaps, but the signs of growing vulnerability are undeniable. The quintessential issue is how much people are still dependent on architecture to live their lives. Fortunately, they still need shelter and they still seek comfort: a major guarantee for relevance. But beyond that it becomes more and more difficult to prove architecture's point. Expressing pride? Urban orientation? An environment for speech and action? Fulfilling people's biological need to build a place? Creating economic value? All debatable, let us say. And one thing is certain: no profession has been decimated more easily than architecture by the current recession. What does that tell us?

So the timeless question has become dramatically topical. Does cultural relevance reside in beauty, in the exception, in the supreme power of design? Or is this the time to devote ourselves entirely to that other ultimate quality that overcomes even the harshest judgement: performance?

For the sake of clarity, may I suggest a new primordial post-crisis criterion for the next award cycle? Namely, resolve.

Ole Bouman, Creative Director of the Shenzhen Biennale, is the former Director of the Nederlands Architectuurinstituut NAi and he formed part of the jury for the 2009 and 2011 editions.

Welfare Architecture: The Public Strikes Back

Fulvio Irace

(2009)

The 340 entries for the 2009 edition bear irrefutable witness to the fact that the European Union Prize for Contemporary Architecture - Mies van der Rohe Award is the most reliable and up-to-date observatory of the European Union's architectural status. The experts and architects' associations who make the nominations, a jury that thoroughly represents very different and varied cultures, and the Mies van der Rohe Foundation headquarters in Barcelona together provide a detailed x-ray of a landscape unified by a twofold (economic and social) destiny, but whose unification does not make it uniform and standardised in representing its needs and cultural traditions.

Talking about architecture 'Made in Europe' is not the same as talking about European architecture. Whereas the latter's typecast interpretation is found in the institutional buildings of its capitals – Strasbourg and Brussels – the reality of individual nations shows a wide variety of themes and solutions that abstracts any attempt to define the character of an alleged European identity.

This contrast is further strengthened by the rich architectural production of the most recent members of the European Union, whose switch from the collectivist economies of the past to the free market economies of today has released fresh energies that represent the undisputed novelty of the new European landscape. Characteristics such as being accustomed to dealing with limited budgets; concern for social and welfare problems; and the rejection of monumental structures because of their pompous symbolism of an overwhelming and intrusive State are mirrored in works offering a previously unseen fresh approach, which coupled with the ability to translate the practical issues of communities who are striving to improve their quality of life is developing into a formally strong and incisive style.

The result is a truly refreshed and renovated portrait of architecture's role as a tool to modify and build new scenarios. After the last decade's euphoria, spectacularisation of construction and careless employment of unlimited budgets for highly scenographic works, the time has come for a return to architecture that is sensitive to social problems and is a means by which to solve needs, leading to the difficult passage from a reckless liberalist economy to a new set of rules in which the State resumes its key role.

An age of great expectations had left on the ground a handful of buildings with a great formal impact, in tune with a society in which transition from industrial to post-industrial looked like the easy transition to a society free from need and craving only entertainment and opulence. Today this age is gone and the brilliant buildings that we saw in the past editions of the award seem removed witnesses of a world gone for good that is very uncongenial to the new modern sensitivity.

The daunting formal performances and the astonishing technological prowess of ensembles like the BMW Welt in Munich or the Porsche Museum in Stuttgart in the 2009 award cycle are admirable examples. With respect to themes apparently more 'low key' or strictly functional in nature – like the Metal Recycling Plant in Odpad Pivka, Slovenia; the Water Filtration Plant in Sant'Erasmo, Venice; the Parking Garage in Coesfeld-Lette, Germany; La Rioja Technology Transfer Centre in Logrono, Spain; and the Nordpark Cable Railway in Innsbruck, Austria – it is possible to see the reflections of a modernity which, like at the turn of the 20th century, meditates about itself and about its role as a pacesetter for a new age.

This year's Prize was therefore able to capture all the signs of change and testify to the presence in Europe of a new design climate in which citizens' welfare is once again becoming essential for architects. Welfare is public by definition; it implies the proactive presence of the State as the key figure of transformation. This, in practice, means that the works commissioned to architects are collective works, community facilities, and social/welfare buildings managed by public institutions. All of this requires also the redefinition, now with a positive connotation, of the word 'collectivity', which had lost much of its value in the decades of global liberalism. The effects of this rebirth are evident, for example, in the revival of design projects related to housing and sustainability. On these issues, architectural research in the last quarter of a century had gone missing. The turn of the 20th and 21st centuries will be remembered for the birth and blooming of museums, the revival of iconic architecture and the abundance of concert halls and other leisure areas, but certainly not for new housing concepts or for attention to urban mobility and transportation infrastructural systems.

But now the city demands, once again, the attention it deserves and the community, in particular, asks for measures and plans that emphasise the city's inherent character as a collective meeting place, until now devalued and hampered by the substantial privatisation of public space by shopping malls and consumerism-oriented leisure areas.

The five finalist projects, over which the jury members were unanimous, tell the storey of these transformations, showing, as in the case of the Zenith Music Hall in Strasbourg, how even the topic of youth culture and music as a leisure activity may be part of a socially-oriented and aesthetically-elaborated plan, while proposing a new building type and an unusual iconography (a 'light' coliseum) for a building traditionally serialised in nature.

Most of the selected projects are dominated by a new concern for urbanity. Gone are the isolated sculptures or landmarks planted in a wasteland, and in their place there are well-detailed projects that reconnect urban volumes, functions and spaces: the Oslo Opera

House, with its emphasis on the idea of collective space; the Luigi Bocconi University that generously opens up its inside spaces to Milan; the Library, Senior Citizen's Centre and Public Space, featuring a courageous proposal of reoccupying an inner courtyard of a city block in Barcelona; and the Nice Tramway Terminal, a vital hub for a public transportation policy focused on the pedestrianisation of the city centre. All of them are harbingers of a return of the project to its original role of transformation, as a governance tool that helps the State, public institutions and administrations in carrying out their duties of respect and support for the community.

The award-winner, the Oslo Opera House and the Emerging Architect Special Mention given to Lea Pelivan and Toma Plejić of Studio Up for the Gymnasium in Koprivnica, Croatia, represent the Prize's ability to understand the signs of change and to create a benchmark for monitoring the new agenda of architecture in Europe.

A professor at the Politecnico di Milano, Fulvio Irace is the former architecture curator of the Triennale di Milano. He was a member of the 2009 award jury.

Three Ways to Public Space
Ewa P. Porębska
(2013)

For the first time in the twenty-five-year-long history of the European Union Prize for Contemporary Architecture - Mies van der Rohe Award, as many as three designs for public spaces in cities have made it to the shortlist of finalists. True, previous winners and finalists of the Award usually served public functions, but this time we are dealing with urban planning rather than with a building intervention.

Does it mean that the organisers and members of the jury have shifted their interest in a new direction? No. But it points to a greater importance and quality of recently developed or modernised public spaces in European cities. It is here, on accessible, attractive, and often innovative sites that the ‹spirit of the times› of the beginning of the 21st century reveals itself, pointing to the potential of cultural and social DIVERSITY.

'Sameness stultifies the mind; diversity stimulates and expands it' says Richard Sennet, a sociologist who studies social ties in cities.[1] A similar sentiment transpires from the European Union documents: 'There are strong links to be exploited between the diversity and social and territorial cohesion of a city and its economic competitiveness and attractiveness; diversity is about culture, identity, history and heritage. People form the core of cities; cities need to be designed for all citizens and not just for the elite, for the tourists, or for the investors.'[2]

Diversity understood in this way occurs in the sphere of a concrete, unique place: the sphere of its history so far, the existing spatial forms, the present economic and political situation, and local habits. Each particular place has its own specific features, its COMPLEXITY.

Diversity as a guideline, and complexity as a point of reference. Three public spaces: Superkilen (Copenhagen), Market Hall (Ghent) and Metropol Parasol (Seville), finalists of the 2013 Prize, provide an inspiring example of this kind of thinking. Three sites, three stories – and three different ways of designing.

Copenhagen – Superkilen/Face to Face with Strangers
According to Eurostat, about 6.6% of the EU population consists of people who are not citizens of their country of residence.[3] Denmark is not particularly outstanding as to the proportion of its foreign citizens, but it does have areas where immigrants from beyond the Western cultural sphere amount to more than half of all residents.[4] These areas, more often than not feature a high crime and unemployment rate and are the focus of special governmental and local programs (such as 'VI KBH'R' –'We the People of Copenhagen'). Their aim is mostly to integrate ethnic minorities, promote intellectual dialogue and prevent minority groups from becoming radicalised.[5]

1. 'A Flexible City of Strangers', Le Monde Diplomatique, 2001, http://mondediplo.com/2001/02/16cities
2. 'Cities of tomorrow. Challenges, visions, ways forward', © European Union Regional Policy, 2011, http://ec.europa.eu/regional_policy/sources/docgener/studies/pdf/citiesoftomorrow/citiesoftomorrow_final.pdf
3. Migration and migrant population statistics. Eurostat European Statistical Office, 2013 http://epp.eurostat.ec.europa.eu/statistics_explained/index.php/Migration_and_migrant_population_statistics
4. KOPENHAGA: Oto czarna lista du skich dzielnic, od których lepiej trzyma si daleka, 2012-10-02, http://www.infodania.pl/aktualnosci/w-danii-powstaly-nowe-getta
5. An Integration Program for National Minorities in Copenhagen. Source: Polish Embassy in Copenhagen,

In order to fully understand Superkilen, a new public space in Nørrebro, it is necessary to know its social background. For many years, this multi-ethnic district of Copenhagen was a scene of a conflict between the city authorities and local activists, accompanied by a series of riots, particularly violent in 2007 and provoked by the demolition of the Ungdomhuset ('Youth House') community centre.[6]

The Superkilen project belongs to a partnership programme of the Copenhagen city authorities and the Realdania association, which supports charitable architectural and planning undertakings. Its direct aim was to create in Nørrebro an innovative urban space, which would meet the needs of the ethnically diversified local community. In the broader sense, its purpose was to work out a model serving as an inspiration for innovative solutions in contemporary cities.

Superkilen, a joint achievement of BIG (architects), Topotek1 (landscape architects) and Superflex (a group of artists), occupies three hectares and is 750 metres long (to make it easier to visualise, it is like three fourths of the length of La Rambla between Plaça de Catalunya and the Columbus monument in Barcelona, or more than twice the length of the Red Square in Moscow). It consists of three main areas: the Green Park (a place for picnics, sports, games and walking dogs), the Black Market (a square with a fountain, grill stands and table games), and the Red Square (with cafes, areas for sports, music and culture).

Typical city activities have gained an unusual setting. In a well-publicised action, representatives of 60 nationalities residing in this district chose 108 objects from cities from their countries. These artifacts of sentimental value were copied or bought and transported to Superkilen to make it 'a contemporary, urban version of a universal garden. A sort of surrealist collection of global urban diversity that in fact reflects the true nature of the local neighborhood – rather than perpetuating a petrified image of homogenous Denmark'.[7]

There are swings from Iraq, benches from Brazil, a fountain from Morocco, grills from South Africa and Argentina, a Japanese playground, Norwegian bike stands and English garbage bins, a bus stop from Kazakhstan, a neon sign from Pennsylvania, and even a sewage drain cover from Poland. Small plaques next to them explain the origin of the object, as if in a museum collection. The selection and consultation process was carefully documented. A specially dedicated webpage (superkilen.dk) perpetuated the memory of the participants in the whole process, mythical travels of several 'chosen ones' or those 'whom the gods love' in quest of treasures—artifacts; the far-away countries they originated from, and the 108 objects/symbols, which gave the district a new image.

Here's the beginning of an urban legend, a sort of fairy tale, in which the neighborhood with 'Strangers' or 'Others' (to use Levinas' term) was familiarised due to a pro-communal, vivid

Wspolnota Polska Association site, 2011: http://www.wspolnota-polska.org.pl/index4eac.html?id=msz07_29
6. A conflict between Copenhagen city authorities, and activists occupying the premises made the building in Jagtvej an object of media attention from the mid-1990s to 2008, http://en.wikipedia.org/wiki/Ungdomshuset
7. Source: designers' own description on Superflex Internet site , http://superflex.net/tools/superkilen

and innovative architectural project. Will it be successful? The open-air world museum of urban objects is no rival for the Tivoli in Copenhagen, but does it not resemble an amusement park by its form and populist vocabulary? Strong, striking colours make this area stand out in the traditional city fabric, unequivocally communicating that it is a special zone – in all meanings of the word. But in order to talk about the social dimension of the 'Superkilen effect', this unique spatial experiment must be supported by long-lasting, extra-architectural effort by city authorities and local organisations.

Ghent – Market Hall/Confronted with a Conservation Doctrine

Ghent has 240 thousand inhabitants, and every year is visited by 2 million tourists, attracted by historic architecture and important cultural events: the Ghent Film Festival (one of the largest European film festivals); the Gentse Feesten music and cultural event (famous for its *stroppendragers* parade with ropes around their necks, to commemorate the events dating back to 1540); and the Floralies Gantoises flower festival (held every five years in the area of the 1913 EXPO World Exhibition).

This Belgian city is well preserved and restored, but that does not mean it has not changed over the years. At the beginning, and then again in the middle of the 20th century, fragments of buildings adjacent to the main monuments marking the Old Town area – Saint Bavo's cathedral (with a Hubertus and Jan van Eyck triptych), St Nicolas's church, and the Belfort bell tower – were demolished. The areas thus vacated became parking lots. In 1996, the city announced an architectural competition for an underground parking garage next to the city hall, but the winning design was never constructed due to public protests. However, another competition entry by Robbrecht en Daem and Marie-José van Hee, though rejected by the jury, served as a basis for the historic centre's new functional programme. This design team won a later competition for a series of squares making up the main historic route in the city, and the construction of a multi-purpose structure with a market hall. Open spaces combine to form a sequence of interwoven stone and green landscapes, connected by a basalt pavement providing proper exposure to the monuments. The new, intentionally modest structure on the square has a light wooden roof covered by glass shingles; depending on the light, it sparkles and changes its appearance. Although this building's form does not refer directly to the surrounding historic buildings, there is some connection apparent in the form of roof gables and the colour scheme.

The area of the project – three hectares – is the same as in Superkilen, but the context and purpose are different. Cultural continuity is particularly important for this rich city with strong burgher and university traditions; this means arranging and complementing the space in a subtle way, with respect for the majestic monuments. In the case of the Market Hall, this tactful subtlety does not translate into architectural humility, and this is probably the reason why the local opinion is split over the new structure. A large scale of the new building standing just next to the bell tower, which is included in the UNESCO World Heritage List, met with criticism on the part of conservative-minded milieus.[8] Is acceptance for the new project possible? Is it just a matter of time? *Sapere aude* (dare to use your wisdom) says the principle followed at the Ghent University. In the context of the Market Hall, let's quote St. Augustine: 'Patience is the companion to wisdom'.

Seville – Metropol Parasol/An Icon in Crisis

'The crisis has demolished the star building, and on its site modesty and shame are beginning to grow'[9] wrote economist and writer Vincente Verdú in *El Pais* about the congress entitled *Mas por Menos* (More for Less), organised in Pamplona in 2010 and devoted to the post-crisis future of architecture. The economic crisis of recent years was acutely felt in the construction industry and real estate market, causing many costly architectural investments to be dropped, particularly in Spain. '... the mother country of the "Bilbao effect" might ultimately be its resting ground'[10] wrote architectural critic David Cohn in his article titled ominously *The Death of the Icon*. He sees instances of this trend in the growing criticism of expensive architectural undertakings, such as the City of Culture in Santiago de Compostela (Peter Eisenman) and the City of Arts and Sciences in Valencia (Santiago Calatrava), but also in the discontinuation of the construction of Zaha Hadid's university library in Seville, a conflict surrounding the construction of Cesar Pelli's Torre Cajasol tower in the same city, and political trials and tribulations over the functioning of Oscar Niemeyer's International Cultural Center in Avilés.

Against such a background, the Metropol Parasol, the structure on Plaza de la Encarnation in the center of Seville open in 2011 and costing € 90 million, seems to be one of the last architectural icons built at the beginning of the 21st century. Designed by Jurgen Mayer H.'s team, it is considered to be the largest wooden architectural structure in the world. It covers almost the entire square – an open platform for events, and a roof over exposed Roman ruins underneath. Restaurants and cafes, retail areas, a panoramic terrace and footbridges take up four levels. Due to technological problems caused by this innovative form, construction was delayed and it much exceeded the planned costs. The structure was financed through a public-private ownership, and one of the largest Spanish building companies, Sacyr Vallehermoso, got a 40-year long concession for its use.[11] High construction costs, a long-term private management and the unusual form, aggressive towards its historic surroundings, caused violent disputes during the prolonged construction process. Nevertheless, Metropol Parasol has become the most recognisable contemporary tourist attraction of the city, and the neglected area, which was used as a parking lot since the 1970s, is now a multi-purpose public space, which generates new workplaces and has become a centre of everyday life for the local people.

8. "Ghent market hall causes controversy", Flanders Today, De Morgen, 30 Aug 2012, http://www.mediargus. be/flanderstoday.admin.en/rss/49951426.html?via=rss&language=en&utm_source=buffer&buffer_share=5e64a
9. 'More for Less: Congress on the State of Architecture', *The Viev from Madrid*, June 2010, http:// viewfrommadrid.blogspot.com/2010/06/more-for-less-congress-on-state-of.html
10. David Cohn, 'The Death of the Icon', *The Architectural Review* , November 2011 ,Vol. 230, http://www. architectural-review.com/view/the-death-of-the-icon/8621628.article
11. Rowan Moore, 'Metropol Parasol, Seville by Jürgen Mayer H – review', The Observer, March 2011, http://www.guardian.co.uk/artanddesign/2011/mar/27/metropol-parasol-seville-mayer-review

Yet, in the words of Francisco Gonzales de Canales in *Domus*, 'There is no reason why public spaces should be just a place for enjoying aperitifs and cappuccinos, but they will only reveal their full depth and plenitude as democratic spaces when citizens voluntarily choose them to do so.'[12] Soon after its official opening, the transformed Plaza de Encarnación became a good illustration of such opinion. In May 2011, Spanish youth protesting against the economic and political situation in the country gathered on this very square.

Why was Parasol chosen to be the site of the gathering? As a sign of excess in these times of crisis? Because of its location? Or maybe it gave enough shade in hot weather? Regardless of the reason, it proved its practical worth as a centre of events. The protest gave this space a meaningful, symbolic dimension.

Copenhagen, Ghent and Seville each have had a different history, different design guidelines and a different social and cultural context. What connects these three new public spaces?

All are a result of competitions, all were commissioned by city authorities and were designed by architects. They all deal with a large urban scale, redevelopment of very important areas, which were more or less neglected for years. Although their purposes varied (Superkilen – integration of a diverse community; Ghent – regulation and complementation of a historic district; Seville – revitalisation of a neglected part of the city, creation of a tourist attraction), they all are multi-functional and open to multiple interpretations and actions, proving themselves just as well in everyday, as in exceptional and unforeseen situations.

They all are unique in shape and strong in expression, which makes the new elements stand out in their surroundings. Here are designs, which unambiguously identify the place and times when they were born. The daring of these architectural and urban forms has provoked many a controversy. Extreme opinions – of rapture or outrage – were voiced in the media, on the Internet, in marches of protest or at happenings.

Such spontaneous and emotional reactions are a visible proof of a growing social interest in the public space, increased awareness of its significance, and thus – of ever greater expectations as to its role and form. They also express people's awareness that they have a right to participate in the shaping of this space, because it provides a field open to actions by various groups, formal and informal, sensitive to the needs of variegated communities. This does not mean solely a participation in top-directed, planned, large and official urban projects. More and more often, grassroots initiatives, communal actions and small-scale movements have their say and manifest themselves in ephemeral, temporary structures, responding to the needs of the moment.

This is the time when the public space ceases to be controlled by politicians, and its shape decided by authoritarian verdicts of professionals.

12. Francisco González de Canales, 'Magic Mushrooms', *Domus*, August 2011, http://www.domusweb.it/en/architecture/2011/07/02/magic-mushrooms.html

Ewa P. Porębska is the editor-in-chief of *Architektura-murator* and was a jury member for the 2013 Prize.

The Dawn of Demos

Kent Martinussen

(2013)

On this 25th anniversary of the European Union Prize for Contemporary Architecture - Mies van der Rohe Award it might hold some significance that three out of the five finalists have the concept of democratic and public space as their predominant focus. And indeed, that the winner, the Harpa Reykjavik Concert Hall and Conference Centre in Iceland, is a mixed-use project that accommodates a variety of public, local and international cultural and commercial activities, as well as a new public plaza and centre for the capital of this legendary island located in the cold northern Atlantic sea.

Could it be that the official European prize for contemporary architecture in its anniversary year is not only reflecting the democratic ideas of Europe but in fact also reevoking the *thelos* of the Barcelona Pavilion that has been the pivot for this award for twenty-five years?

The German Pavilion, which was designed by Ludwig Mies van der Rohe for the 1929 Barcelona International Exhibition, is a remarkable piece of architecture. Having been reconstructed in 1986, this iconic building can again be admired for its free plan and open space and perhaps in particular, for its beautiful minimalistic design and attention to detail.

Interestingly enough the building had no real programme, as clients and architects would understand the term today. Its function was to be the scenario of the official reception presided over by King Alfonso XIII of Spain and the German authorities at the exhibition opening.

In designing the Barcelona Pavilion, Mies van der Rohe chose not to create an exhibition space but rather to exhibit *a* space. Embodying the mental model of the new Weimar republic, the Barcelona Pavilion was a space that captured the idea of a new dawn of a truly pacifist and democratic era for Germany, replacing the aggressive and authoritarian empire that had fared so badly in World War I.

When it was originally built in 1929, the Barcelona Pavilion was a shocking ensemble of free-floating spaces that enabled the visitor to claim the space and stage him or herself as the protagonist of a partly dematerialised reality that was about boarderlessness, free flow and interaction among people, ideas and physical space.

The Barcelona Pavilion is a nonrepresentational space that allows for one single conventional figure, namely the bronze statue by the sculptor Georg Kolbe, which by no accident is named *The Dawn*: architecture as well as democracy was stretching out as it was awakening for the new dawn of Germany.

To a great extent, the idea of 'society' has been, at least in the case of Europe, about democracy – about the idea that an ordinary person is a respected and emancipated being who cannot be reduced to a mere number in the labour force.

I think that the Barcelona Pavilion is more about being the space for such a newly emancipated subject living in an open, peaceful and democratic society, than it is about the sheer mastering of new aesthetics by the architect. The Barcelona Pavilion is about putting the ordinary person not in the middle, but rather off-centre and in the flow of the space. In this way, he or she is freed from the burden of the hegemony of representational space focussed on the power that always has been by definition external to this new kind of person, the emancipated citizen of democracy.

Europe: Architecture and Democracy

There seems to be a historical alliance between architecture and Europe. The idea of democracy – the European governance of our own choice – was legendarily born some 2,500 years ago in the Greek city-state, the Greek *polis*. This is also where the word 'politician' – named after *polis* – was coined and the job defined as being in charge of the caretaking and development of the city and its inhabitants, the people, the *demos*. Since then, the 'job description' has been expanded from taking care of the city to taking care of society.

The idea of the *demos* – the people and their power – was in fact critical for the invention of an array of public programmes that lead to building typologies and other kinds of physical infrastructures, which enable these functions to take place at all. Since the Greeks, and later the Romans, the invention of such typologies has played a major role in the history of European architecture.

And the idea of democracy is not the only reason, but it is certainly one of the most important, that explains why Europe is undoubtedly the region where the broadest range of architectural styles, typologies and artistic expressions has been developed. The point is that the political concept of Europe emerged hand in hand with the birth of the concepts of architecture, the city and its citizens. And thus, the alliance of democracy and cities and architecture makes up the very backbone of the idea of Europe.

Not only in the second half of the 20th century have we seen tremendous architectural accomplishments. In 1923 Le Corbusier coined the saying 'architecture or revolution' meaning that he saw architecture as a way of avoiding revolution by providing proper living facilities for a population living under horrible conditions. World War II derailed his vision, but afterwards more or less all European countries established ministries of housing. As a result, since then certainly Europe has provided 'architecture for the people' meaning the construction of decent housing with running water, plumbing and all of the architectural commodities by which we define the modern democratic welfare state.

This accomplishment is one of the key components in the relative stability and overall growth in Europe for the last fifty to sixty years, during which we have seen society and architecture woven together into the European democratic tradition.

If we zoom back to the Pavilion and the Prize, I believe it is obvious that this democratic understanding of architecture – even on an informal level – was a value that informed the thinking of the jury when we chose the finalists and the winner for the award. The scale, the programmatic content and the aesthetic values were tipped in the direction of Europe and democracy. The finalists all have one very distinct thing in common: they create democratic spaces for public use.

It goes without saying that all the finalists are great pieces of architecture characterised by much attention paid to traditional virtues such as detail and an artistic aesthetic approach. And perhaps the impressive Icelandic Harpa by Henning Larsen Architects, Studio Olafur Eliasson and Batteríið Architects is the strongest proof in these years of difficulty for Europe and the world that architecture should and can exist as both an elevated form of art and a pragmatic component for democracy.

Kent Martinussen is the CEO of the Danish Architecture Center and formed part of the 2013 jury.

Transformations: Europe and European Architecture
Hans Ibelings

In the twenty-five years of the existence of the European Union Prize for Contemporary Architecture - Mies van der Rohe Award, Europe and its architecture have undergone impressive changes. The political landscape was transformed in 1989 by the collapse of Communism in Central and Eastern Europe and the subsequent disappearance of the Iron Curtain that had divided Europe for more than four decades. The Prize was created two years before this crucial year in recent European history, shortly after Spain and Portugal had joined the European Union in 1986.

In 1988, the first award went to a project in the north of Portugal, designed by a Portuguese architect. Austria, Finland and Sweden became members in 1995, and three years later the seventh award was for a building in Austria, designed by a Swiss architect, who slipped through in the limited time slot during which Swiss architects were not excluded from competition, which has otherwise been open only to architects from and projects in EU-member states and countries that are part of the European Economic Space, or candidates and potential candidates for EU membership.

In 2004 the post-communist transformation of Central Europe was marked by the accession to the EU of Slovenia, a number of former Eastern Bloc countries, plus three former Soviet republics, Estonia, Latvia and Lithuania. In 2007 a special mention went to an office in Slovenia. In the same year two more countries joined, Bulgaria and Rumania. The 25th anniversary of the Prize coincides with the year that Croatia has become an EU member. In 2009 a Croatian office got the special mention.

If there is no correlation between political developments and jury decisions, there is at least an interesting parallel, that the extension of the EU, and of the candidate countries, has more than once coincided with awarding prizes to newcomers. Yet there has not been a Central or Eastern European overall winner yet. In the twenty-five years of its existence the winners of the award have always been architects from Western Europe, with projects built in the Western half of the continent, just as none of the eighteen European winners of the Pritzker Prize up until 2013 (London-based Zaha Hadid is counted here as well) has his or her office anywhere east of the Berlin-Vienna line. So no matter how united Europe may be, the balances are still very much tipping to the West.

Even though it is not unlikely the EU will be enlarged again after the accession of Croatia, the Prize's territory cannot expand very much anymore, since nearly every country bar Switzerland and Bosnia Herzegovina is in already. So if the Prize would seek growth, it could only find it outside Europe. The short-lived Latin-American version of the Prize could be reanimated, or an Asian Prize could be created, or a global one, but within Europe the award as it is has reached its geographical limits.

And European architecture has reached a limit as well. The foundation of the Prize was a very timely one. Aside from honouring one exceptional project every two years, the award process has been documenting an extremely rich period of European architecture, which evolved against a background of huge geopolitical changes.

The newest member of the EU, Croatia, did not exist as an independent country when the Prize was founded. Nor did EU member Slovenia for that matter, both of which were still part of the Socialist Federal Republic of Yugoslavia, which would collapse in the chaos of war in the following decade. Estonia, Latvia and Lithuania were still Republics of the Soviet Union, the Czech Republic and Slovakia were one country, and Germany consisted of two, the German Federal Republic and the German Democratic Republic. The youngest architects today had not been born when the Berlin Wall and the Iron Curtain were dividing Europe, or when the Prize was established. This means that for a substantial numbers of professionals in Europe, there has always been a European award for architecture, just as there is no other reality than that of a European Union.

Even in 1988, when keen observers might have been able to witness the first signs of change and to envision the potential impact of Gorbachev's *perestroika*, it was nearly impossible to predict the changes the continent would undergo in the following years. The most educated guess would have been aside reality.

At first sight, architecture has not been changing as drastically as Europe's geopolitical configuration, but if one compares the European architectural landscape of the late 1980s with the situation today there are significant differences. Back then, architecture was very much nationally partitioned. There was definitely an international community of architects as well, but most of the members of this community got commissions only in their own country. Having an international field of action was rare for an architect. That has changed drastically since then, and by any measurement architectural culture has become much more international.

The number of architects with jobs outside their own country grew exponentially, partly thanks to the European tendering for larger public commissions; the Erasmus exchange programmes that started at European universities in 1987 has created a European-scale globalisation of architectural education and has promoted the international mobility of new generations of students and young architects. The subsequent creation of Europe's internal market and the free movement of goods, services, capital and persons, has greatly contributed to an internationalisation of the work force of many offices.

In the late 1980s Postmodernism was still in full bloom. During that time, most projects for the 'critical reconstruction and cautious renewal' of the IBA in West Berlin were finished, or nearing completion. The IBA, which was initiated in 1979, is one of the landmarks of European Postmodernism. Architecturally speaking most projects may have lost the allure they had when they were new (to paraphrase Karl Kraus, they now look dated, but quite likely some will prove to be timeless very soon). Yet, even if the IBA has lost its attraction architecturally speaking, its conceptual urbanistic approach has become an enduring model. The same holds true for the transformation Barcelona underwent before the Olympics of 1992, which reflects a similar renewed interest in urban culture and the cultural aspects of cities.

This cultural dimension is very much part and parcel of Postmodernism. There are many examples of the importance of the cultural side of architecture and urbanism, such as the creation of a number of significant architectural institutions, such as the Ifa in Paris, the DAM in Frankfurt, the NAi in Rotterdam and AzW in Vienna.

The cultural role of architecture was also reflected in the museum building boom in Germany and Mitterrand's *Grands Projets* in France. And obviously, the Prize can been seen as an initiative that fits in this postmodern context with its emphasis on the culture of architecture. The preamble to the award rules states that 'The European space is composed of an emulsion of natural and cultural, vernacular and canonical, traditional and artificial elements. Contemporary architecture must assume this ambiguity, project it towards the future and offset the natural wear to which forms are subject by means of a symmetrical process of innovation, a process that has been presided over by works that, introduced into an architectural tradition, contribute a new inflection or added value that can only be qualified as "artistic".

Without suggesting an inextricable link between the one and the other, the cultural dimension of architecture flourished when the idea of Europe flourished. There have always been Eurosceptics, and there will always be, but part of the history of this award was that it has become an established institution in an atmosphere that was implicitly pro EU and pro Europe, or at least neutral to it. A change in attitude surfaced in 2005, when discontent expressed itself in the referendums that turned down what was wrongly described as a European constitution. Two years later, the banking crisis started a chain reaction of crises that led to the economic, social and political mess Europe has been in since 2008.

Aside from affecting the building industry and architecture in a direct, financial way, the crisis has had an eroding effect on the culture of architecture as well. It would be short-sighted to maintain that it is only the economy, because looking at Europe in a broader time frame, it becomes clear that the current crisis is only one aspect of what the historian Paul Kennedy has described as a watershed in Western history, part of which is that after more than two centuries of rapid population growth, Europe has entered a period of demographic stagnation. Architecture, and the building industry it is part of, will face the consequences of this, since there is a basic equation between an increase of the number of people and the number of extra square metres of built space needed to accommodate the lives of these people.

Demographic stagnation has a detrimental effect on building and architecture. Before the beginning of the demographic revolution around 1750-1800, there were a few architects, who designed the exceptional church, palace or city hall. Since then the number of architects and architectural jobs has risen enormously. Without wanting to rely on rigid determinism, it is not unlikely that Europe's stagnant population will see a dramatic decrease of architecture (and of the number of architects) again, stabilising at a new normal that could be closer to pre 1800 standards than to those of the bustling 19th and 20th centuries.

In certain ways the postmodern relativism of the 1970s and 1980s has been rather prescient, laying a philosophical foundation for the current stagnation. Before Postmodernism there was Modernism, which was based on the industrial idea of growth and progress, of technological modernisation, of development in a particular direction. Postmodernism may at first have seemed like a reaction to Modernism, a counter-movement, but the essence of Postmodernism turned out to be that everything can go in any direction at all, can exist side by side. As such, Postmodernism is a complex form of stagnation, which neatly parallels the stagnation Europe is currently witnessing in many fields.

Postmodernism has been around for quite a while, yet only now is that stagnation becoming obvious. In a review of Hari Kunzru's *Gods Without Men*, published in *The International Herald Tribune* early in 2012, Douglas Coupland described the 21st century as the beginning of an 'aura-free universe in which all eras coexist at once – a state of possibly permanent atemporality given to us courtesy of the Internet. No particular era now dominates. We live in a post-era era without forms of its own powerful enough to brand the times. The *zeitgeist* of 2012 is that we have a lot of *zeit* but not much *geist*. I can't believe I just wrote that last sentence, but it's true.' That same argument had been expounded slightly earlier in *Vanity Fair* by Kurt Andersen in "You Say You Want a Devolution?". Early on he writes: 'Since 1992, as the technological miracles and wonders have propagated and the political economy has transformed, the world has become radically and profoundly new. Here is what's odd: during the same 20 years, the appearance of the world (computers, TVs, telephones, and music players aside) has changed hardly at all, less than it did during any 20-year period for at least a century. The past is a foreign country, but the recent past – the 00s, the 90s, even a lot of the 80s – looks almost identical to the present.' The article concludes: 'We seem to have trapped ourselves in a vicious cycle – economic progress and innovation stagnated, except in information technology; which leads us to embrace the past and turn the present into a pleasantly eclectic for-profit museum; which deprives the cultures of innovation of the fuel they need to conjure genuinely new ideas and forms; which deters radical change, reinforcing the economic (and political) stagnation.'

In 1994 the Marxist historian Eric Hobsbawn published *The Age of Extremes: A History of the World, 1914–1991*. In this he contended that 'the historical forces that shaped the [20th] century, are continuing to operate. We live in a world captured, uprooted and transformed by the titanic economic and techno-scientific process of the development of capitalism, which has dominated the past two or three centuries'. But, he added, 'We know, or at least it is reasonable to suppose, that it cannot go on *ad infinitum*. The future cannot be a continuation of the past, and there are signs, both externally, and, as it were, internally, that we have reached a point of historical crisis'.

Just like there were great churches, city halls and villas built before 1800, there will always be the occasional exceptional architectural object in Europe deserving an award, but it is not too rash to predict that in the light of current economic, demographic and cultural stagnation, the pool to choose from will become smaller in the future. This statement is of course based on the assumption that it will still be architecture as we know it right now. But that may not be the case. It might also be that architecture and architects are going to adapt to the conditions of a new normal after two centuries of growth and progress, and will develop a new self-definition and maybe even a new ethos of the profession.

During the last decade there were already many signs hinting at such a redefinition of what architecture and architects could be, or could become. And this shift can eventually challenge and change the concept of the EU Prize for Contemporary Architecture - Mies van der Rohe Award, which is currently a prize for an outstanding singular architectural object, which can be credited to an individual architect or office.

If just one edition of the award suffices to see signs of a change, the 2013 finalist projects seem to hint at a possible new direction, of architecture, and the Prize. Three out of the five finalist projects are not just a building, but something that could only be described in more general terms as urban interventions. These types of projects could be the beginning of opening up the Prize to different types of architecture, beyond the individual object that might fit its context but exists in splendid isolation. There is obviously a wealth of new practices, in which architecture is moving away from designing objects into the direction of social design, spatial agencies and all kind of intervention strategies and transformation processes within the existing urban fabric and built substance.

Hans Ibelings was the co-founder and editor-in-chief of the magazine *A10* and has recently launched *The Architecture Observer*.

Juries, Awards and Concepts: Why We Need to Give Prizes

Pau de Solà-Morales

I.

The relative importance of architecture awards when it comes to fostering the advancement and development of the discipline is hard to assess. It might seem that the establishment of an award, with its periodical, repetitive mechanics of appointing a jury and issuing a verdict, is an event of little significance other than that of glorifying the winners. In this context, the 25th anniversary of the European Union Prize for Contemporary Architecture - Mies van der Rohe Award provides us with a suitable opportunity to reflect on the need for and usefulness of this social ritual to which, as a rule, we do not attach too much importance.

To do so however, we must understand, first, the relative situations of each of the agents involved and comprehend their diachronic perspective. Needless to say, each edition of an award presupposes a set of fixed elements: the projects presented, their creators, the members of the jury and the institution of the award. The jury, composed in general of professionals of greater or lesser prestige and merit, is faced with a line-up of projects generated almost at the same time as the verdict is required. Although the jury members' knowledge and professional experience may be very wide, they have only a reduced temporal perspective of the works, and critical assessment of architecture needs time to mature. The *critical* appraisal of the projects is thereby permanently limited and, consequently, conditioned by values and phenomena relating to the present moment. Indeed, the members of the jury, lacking those critical mechanisms of judgement, will find relationships between the projects and their immediate environment, either spatial or mental: on some occasions they will find an aspect of a project interesting, or notable, by virtue of its immediate link to some recent event; on other occasions, by virtue of its formal or visual proximity to other comparable projects of especial significance; and on other occasions, they will simply find other issues of interest in the projects.

Nonetheless, besides being the *winner* of an award or a competition, what makes a project significant (that is, also *worthy* of the prize), should be its importance on the disciplinary level: how will this project be regarded from a temporal distance, when considerations relating specifically to the current moment no longer apply? Will it be looked upon as an important, influential, significant project, or will it just disappear into the overall anonymity of city buildings? Will it be inscribed in the annals of historical architectural landmarks or will it become a mere anecdote on the sidelines of the History of Architecture (with capital letters)? And on the more practical side, how many other architects will contemplate, study and learn from it? How many professionals, albeit inadvertently, will modify their cognitive mechanisms and, by extension, their design methods, as the result of having observed a building?

In his introductory text for the inaugural Mies van der Rohe Award, Kenneth Frampton, an acknowledged contemporary architecture historian and theorist and Chairman of the first jury, provides an overview of each of the nominee buildings. Having mentioned that for once, since this was the first edition of the award, the evaluation period had been somewhat longer than the two years stipulated in the rules, the author attempts to classify the selected entries in a set of major categories: 'high-tech', 'neo-rationalist', 'contextualist', 'minimalist', 'structuralist' and even 'neo-historicist'. In this set of *labels* we recognise the indelible mark of the author, who in his long career as an architecture critic has engaged in separating out, classifying and designating buildings and styles and with meticulous care has explained the meaning, though approximate and somewhat imprecise, of each of these CONCEPTS.

Indeed, the *critic* of architecture, like the philosopher (from Plato to Deleuze and Guattari), creates *concepts*, and uses these concepts as 'models of interpretation and explanation of the world'. Concepts which, at the same time, are fruit of experience, of discerning, intelligent work and of periodical and continuous contemplation of reality; and also comprehension mechanisms of the surroundings, without which there would not be even the remotest possibility of endowing reality with meaning. Concepts, therefore, that structure and direct our thought, subtly interceding in our perception and appreciation of architectural phenomena.

II.

In this same text, Frampton provides us with a number of guidelines regarding the present and future not only of European but also of much of global architecture, which unfortunately seems to have been sailing for some time on a sea of undefined, amorphous concepts. During Classicism, and even during the legendary period of Modern Architecture, a set of strong, clear, unitary concepts ('reason', 'machine', 'order', 'progress', 'geometry', etc.) was established and historiography undertook the task of describing and naming them. Contemporary architecture, however, whose only *raison d'être* would seem to be the constant renovation of style (in which each new concept seeks to eclipse its immediate forerunner), has apparently lost its way. This is clear in the disparity of styles, a disparity that observers like Frampton attempt to pin down in an endless stream of *isms* that succeed each other hotfoot. The selection of nominees for each edition of the Mies van der Rohe Award is evidence of this: otherwise, how could Gae Aulenti's Musée d'Orsay coexist in the same selection with the Borges e Irmão Bank by Álvaro Siza? How can we consider and compare Richard Rogers's Lloyd's Bank in London and Rafael Moneo's Museo de Mérida?

The total absence of clear referents in architecture has contributed to the fact that style is no longer primordial and has lost its attributes as canon, guide or model. The outcome is a culture where 'anything goes' in formal terms, which results in the most ridiculous of mannerisms. We might ingenuously believe that the problem lies in the fact that critics, from whom we borrow conceptual structures, have not yet come up with the suitable terms and definitions by which we may make sense of the most recent architecture. But it seems, rather, that contemporary architecture, not only in Europe but practically throughout the entire world, is no longer a unitary discipline governed by clear notions sustained by those conceptual platforms that Deleuze called *plateaux*. On the contrary, we are in the presence of a fragmented architecture based on the moment (on the event), a liquid architecture, lacking in clear points of reference, in which the designer and the critic have no alternative other than to formulate concepts *ad hoc* because existing concepts are no longer reusable at a later moment. Álvaro Siza has said that 'any design is an earnest endeavour to capture the nuances of a given instant in a transient reality'. To capture the fragility and the transience of the moment, of the place, of the client, of the context. Subtle, fleeting relations for an architecture of ephemeral, volatile criteria.

III.

Nonetheless, the fleeting and somewhat banal nature of contemporary architecture should not discourage either award organisers or architecture critics. Somewhat paradoxically, architecture prizes are important, and their importance lies precisely in the fact that they confer stability, structure and a sensation of permanence on a discipline that seems to have been lacking in these qualities for some time. Architecture has apparently lost credibility on almost all fronts: academic (did you know that many countries are considering removing architecture schools from the university system?); research ('research' has been confused with entirely frivolous 'fantasy'); disciplinary (who would still rely on the criteria of an architect when it comes to designing the layout of a house or a city, when we have engineers and lawyers, who really *are* serious?!); professional (there have been thousands of cases in which astronomical quotations or technical errors have been received by their authors with arrogant smirks and comments); and mediatic (the time has passed in which architects competed with each other to feature in the latest Discovery Channel documentaries, with titles like *Megastructures*). In reference to digital architecture (though applicable to any other sphere of media architecture), Bernard Cache has said that 'despite all our precautions (…) it is now entirely evident that the digital in architecture has become a game for adolescents who dream of building a pretty object, whatever its economic or social cost'.

Fortunately for us, joint disciplinary effort and mutual *inter pares* recognition constitute one of the few remaining guarantees of stability. In a context of total conceptual instability, so distorted by the mass media and by appearances, it is precisely awards that contribute towards building an orderly discourse of legitimacy, albeit weak and ephemeral. For as prize-winners, those architects and those buildings will obtain a 'plus' in terms of media significance, in the midst of deafening noise, and thanks to this extra significance, those architects and those buildings will be contemplated and studied with a substantial degree of serenity by the few who still appreciate good architecture.

At a time of confusion and perplexity, we cannot expect the emergence *ex nihilo* of a set of structures that will immediately structure our perception of the world. This messianic vision tends to confuse work well done and the culture of effort with the vanity of recognition by the media and quick success. In essence, concepts are merely social consensus. Interaction between many people and professionals, the generation of consensuses and, in the last instance, the emergence of a predominant common paradigm and of agreement between the different parties are needed in order to generate the concepts that might structure, organise and criticise architecture of the future. *Roma die uno non aedificata est* ('Rome wasn't built in a day').

Award-winning works with pedigree, with tradition and seriousness, independent and constant, will stand out by virtue of these qualities over and above the mass of formless ideas, and they will last much longer over time. The institutionalisation of a ritual, the gathering of experts and the selection of one or several exceptional works, together with their periodical reproduction, will constitute the basis for an incipient discourse which, like that of critics, will help to create concepts where only confusion formerly reigned.

It isn't much, but it's better than nothing. Perhaps the jury members lack the historical and critical perspectives they need to evaluate the competition entries; perhaps they lack a set of valid, lasting criteria or concepts; perhaps they are unaware of the long-term importance of their work. Nonetheless, it is on their independence and honesty that the future form of European Architecture may depend.

Pau de Solà-Morales is a professor at the Escola Tècnica Superior d'Arquitectura de Reus.

Living Well, Within Global Limits: What Role for European Architecture?
Sarah Mineko Ichioka

Landmark dates can help to focus the mind. The 25th anniversary of the European Union Prize for Contemporary Architecture - Mies van der Rohe Award coincides with another important occasion: the first time in human history that levels of atmospheric carbon have exceeded 400 parts per million. Climate scientists have long warned that 350ppm was the upper safety limit for the maintenance of a terrestrial climate conducive to human life[1]. And climate instability is only the most urgent symptom of the strain our current way of life is placing on our planet. So, while there are many angles from which one could contemplate the future of European architecture, I will focus my thoughts along one path: the role architecture (and of an elite prize that champions it) might play in ensuring the sustainability of the European city in a globalised world.

Sustainability is a pertinent area for contemplation in planning the future of the Prize, since its own organisers celebrate it as a 'platform for investigation, development and implementation of sustainable architectural practices that promote the social, cultural and economic benefits of sustainable growth'[2]. With such a stated focus, one might expect chagrin for the years when mammoth convention centres and museum-shrines to luxury sports cars were considered as prize contenders; but sustainability can be defined in different ways. Reviewing the Prize's twenty-five-year record, it seems to focus on continuity and canon-building, both worthy aims but ones aligned more with certain aspects of the term 'sustainable'—'able to be maintained at a certain rate or level' or 'able to be upheld or defended'[3]. The area where the Prize offers much potential to grow in future is in the celebration of projects for how they conserve 'an ecological balance by avoiding depletion of natural resources'[4]; the post-Brundtland Commission sense of meeting 'the needs of current generations without compromising the ability of future generations to meet their own needs'[5].

Europe, as the rest of the world, has entered a period of increasing extremes including income inequality and political polarisation. Demagogues will always exploit socio-economic instability to whip up xenophobic and protectionist sentiments, but rather than worrying about an imagined tide of immigrants desperate to exploit its welfare systems, Europe must consider its position in a world where the locus of economic and cultural influence is steadily shifting

With thanks to Elias Redstone, Michael Ichioka and Jack Stiller for their comments.

1. Justin Gillis, "Heat-Trapping Gas Passes Milestone, Raising Fears," *New York Times,* May 11, 2013: A1
2. Fundació Mies van der Rohe. "Foreword" in *2011 European Union Prize for Contemporary Architecture,* ed. Diane Gray (Barcelona: Actar, 2012), 4.
3. Entry for 'sustainable'. Oxford Online Dictionary (Oxford: Oxford University Press, 2013) http://oxforddictionaries.com/definition/english/sustainable
4. Ibid.
5. Kaj Barlund, "Sustainable development concept and action" in *Publications* (Geneva: United Nations Economic Commission for Europe Information Service: 2004) http://www.unece.org/oes/nutshell/2004-2005/focus_sustainable_development.html

to the south and east.[6] Just a few examples of the many impacts of emerging global power shifts on cities include: the flush of investment in prime real estate in European capitals by East and West Asian investors, from private individuals driving up house prices, to sovereign wealth funds making game-changing, urban-scale investments; and the reverse brain drain of countries to their former colonies, as skilled young people abandon slowing European cities to seek opportunity in the burgeoning capitals of South America and Africa.

But no challenge threatens the existence of European cities more than the current late capitalist system's disregard for the natural limits of our planet. The geographic disparities of habitability that anthropogenic climate instability is predicted to create across Europe[7] overlap significantly with disparities of recent economic fortune: many of the southern areas most crippled by the crash of speculative real estate markets and governmental regimes of austerity will also be rendered less hospitable than their natural resource-rich or industry-rich cousins in the north.

Some might argue that an architectural prize may have little impact on these wider concerns, given that so much of the contemporary built environment is constructed without the direct involvement of architects, let alone the type who win international awards. What impact can individual buildings have on the sustainability of lifestyles at the urban scale, especially as the metrics might differ when surveyed across cities and regions with diverse economies, cultures and challenges? Protesting that one's sphere of influence is limited is not sufficient excuse to exert no influence at all. As some experts consider the carbon threshold we have just exceeded a point of no return, the stakes and urgency are of the essence; arguably comparable to those of a world war[8]. As in wartime, every institution and individual must play its part.

The Prize is awarded to enforce European cultural identity's manifestation in buildings and spaces, celebrating 'architecture's role as both a basis for the interchange of ideas as well as a unifying element that defines a common European culture'[9], its contribution to 'the construction of the European city'[10]. Historically, the Prize has tended to focus on a particular category of 'culture' that is tied to image-making, cultural consumption, and the leisure economy. Although the longer list of commended projects has been reasonably diverse

6. See, for example: Richard Dobbs et al, *Urban world: Cities and the rise of the consuming class* (City of publication unknown: McKinsey Global Institute, 2012).
7. European Environment Agency, *Climate Change Impacts and Vulnerability in Europe 2012: An indicator-based report* (Luxembourg: Office for Official Publications of the European Union, 2012) doi:10.2800/66071
8. Laurence L. Delina and Mark Diesendorf "Is wartime mobilisation a suitable policy model for rapid national climate mitigation?" in *Energy Policy*, 58 (2013), 371-380.
9. Fundació Mies van der Rohe. "European Union Prize for Contemporary Architecture Mies van der Rohe Award Rules" in *2011 European Union Prize for Contemporary Architecture*, ed. Diane Gray (Barcelona: Actar, 2012),16.
10. Ibid 4.

over time, including schools, housing, transport, etc., there is a preponderance of cultural buildings amongst the winners. This instrumentalisation of buildings as a means of projecting the importance of certain categories of European culture relates to broader campaigns of government-led investment in the cultural sector as a post-industrial economic alternative. The cover image of the 2011 catalogue depicts a few tourists taking photographs of ancient marbles in the pristine setting of the Neue National Gallery; the prizewinner as cultural spectacle, focused on the sophisticated display of the past. The 2013 awardees continue this tendency: the winner is a concert hall, and the emerging architect award is for a music academy. These cultural buildings are attractive, sophisticated, well crafted; they are also easily deployed as tools of urban, national or corporate branding and as magnets for tourism.

How might the reinterpretation of European cultural identity and reassessment of its values—as channelled through the medium of architecture—contribute to the sustainability of our cities, and the broader world? Promisingly, the Prize is intended to 'detect and highlight' works 'whose innovative character acts as an orientation or even a manifesto'[11]. The official architectural prize of the brave and contested political and economic alliance that is the European Union will inevitably have as one of its aspects a propagandistic or promotional function. This aspect should be openly embraced; leading us to ask which characteristics of European architecture the Prize should actively seek to export. The positioning of the Prize as a manifesto holds significant potential, but it must exceed the important yet insufficient criteria of formal beauty, cultural reference, and experiential delight to meet the urgent, existential demands of the present. *So where should the compass point? What broader social and behavioural changes do we want to see manifest in our buildings and cities? More difficult, but essential to ask: which of these changes must we enact to ensure our very survival?*

In the new reality we face, 'sustainable' architecture should be defined as that which can readily adapt to unstable conditions, whether flash floods or extreme heat, whereas 'excellent' architecture (that which deserves award) should be recognised as that which actively mitigates the causes of climate instability, replenishes natural resources, and accordingly supports our species' transition to the other side of what environmentalist Paul Gilding calls 'the Great Disruption', the crisis that will ensue when the planet's natural limits are exceeded, forcing us to rapidly and thoroughly reimagine our way of life[12].

We humans need to adjust our buildings, our cities, and our lifestyles to a level of resource consumption that fits the one planet we've got, and that means consuming a lot less than we do now. The Prize is intended to underscore the 'essential relationship between quality of life

11. Ibid16.
12. Paul Gilding, *The Great Disruption: How the Climate Crisis Will Transform the Global Economy* (London: Bloomsbury, 2011).

and quality of the environment'[13]. *What new potentials could the Prize unleash if it accepts that 'sustainable growth', a tenet of its current constitution and a stock platitude across sectors, is in fact an oxymoron? What if it adopts the position that award criteria must favour new social models? What could award-winning architecture for a post-Disruption, steady state, restorative economy look like?*

Retrofitting and the conservation of embodied energy of existing components and structures are important elements of sustainable architecture, and a chief criterion for sustainability amongst past prize-winners has been their durability, and in some cases their reuse of materials. This approach is exemplified by 2011 emerging architecture laureate Bet Capdeferro's statements about 'being conscious of our own temporality' in relation to the reinterpretation of existing structures[14], and that 'buildings that have been designed in complicity with the environment are more capable of being reused and are more capable of resisting the passage of time'[15]. Since the vast majority of the premiated buildings have been new-build projects, the potential of new technologies—e.g. building information modelling and networked technologies, which allow for building performance monitoring and responsive management, and biomimetic and cradle-to-cradle approaches to design—also bears consideration. In this instance, a useful reference point for the Mies Award organisers is the International Living Future Institute's Living Building Challenge, which sets a rigorous set of standards for buildings 'that operate as cleanly, beautifully and efficiently as nature's architecture'[16].

In addition to traditional public or private clients, those responsible for these new award-worthy projects may be drawn from what research and architecture practice 00:/ have identified as the 'civic economy'. 00:/ define this emergent economy as 'people, ventures and behaviours that fuse innovative ways of doing from the traditionally distinct spheres of civil society, the market, and the state. Founded upon social values and goals, and using deeply collaborative approaches to development, production, knowledge sharing and financing, [it] generates goods, services and common infrastructures that neither the state nor the market economy alone have been able to accomplish.'[17] New economic structures for generating and funding architecture could include crowdsourcing platforms, cooperative models of finance, and the

13. Ibid.16.
14. Fundació Mies van der Rohe. "The Reuse of Buildings" in *2011 European Union Prize for Contemporary Architecture*, ed. Diane Gray (Barcelona: Actar, 2012), 23
15. Fundació Mies van der Rohe. "Interview Tarald Lundevall with Ramon Bosch, Bet Capdeferro" in *2011 European Union Prize for Contemporary Architecture*, ed. Diane Gray (Barcelona: Actar, 2012), 70.
16. Living Building Challenge, "Challenging All Comers", (retrieved May 6, 2013) http://living-future.org/lbc
17. 00:/, *Compendium for a New Civic Economy* (London: 00:/, 2011), 9.

Transition Towns model of local microcurrencies[18]. Post-consumer typologies of architecture could include the colonisation of redundant retail units as homes or social enterprises, networked communal workspaces, self-build communities, and public realm transformations initiated by non-profit organisations.

If it evolves to embrace the potentials of qualitative development over quantitative growth, the Prize may need to recalibrate its scope from the discrete building or space to include environmental remediation projects, infrastructural systems, cooperative communities and the like, although this would doubtless face opposition from architectural purists. At an urban scale, it will also need to consider when and where architecture's absence could be stronger than its presence; in some cases strategies of excision, retreat, or even rewilding[19] may be the most responsible design responses.

European cities already enjoy a competitive advantage in some important aspects: their relatively compact built form, the core of which was often conceived pre-fossil fuel, the practice or potential for renewal of localised supply chains, combined with the potentials of participatory democracy offer the potential to envisage a better future through creating aspirational lifestyles for cultural export. On this basis, European soft power cultural diplomacy—including the awarding of transnational prizes—might draw its strength from the celebration of how we live in balance with the planet, tangibly demonstrating the merits of quality-of-life over quantity-of-stuff, in the manner that it has previously successfully commoditised its history or particular strains of high culture. In future, the European city's key to survival may lie in demonstrating thought-leadership and practical expertise in creating post-Disruption solutions, including ecologically restorative and socially innovative design solutions for its built environment.

18. For more information about the Transition Towns Network, see http://www.transitionnetwork.org/
19. Elizabeth Kolbert, Department of Ecology, "Recall of the Wild", *The New Yorker*, December 24, 2012, 50

Sarah Mineko Ichioka is the Director of the Architecture Foundation in London and the Co-Director of the London Festival of Architecture.

The Future
of European
Architecture
Pedro Gadanho

When one wants to consider the future of any form of activity, one is tempted to extrapolate trends from current conditions. One translates signs from the present onto the shape of things to come. The conditions of a given moment, however, may be too circumstantial, and one should be particularly aware of their transient nature. This is the dilemma one obviously faces when considering 'the future of European architecture'.

At the time the European Union Prize for Contemporary Architecture - Mies van der Rohe Award commemorates its 25th anniversary, the European project from which this Prize emanates – and to which it owes its symbolic meaning and promoting purpose – is itself at a crossroads.

In between austerity measures, the South and North divide, growing unemployment, a feeling of impoverishment and insecurity, and the apparent unsustainability of the Welfare State model, which had given the region prosperity after World War II, Europe itself seems to be facing a pivotal, if transient moment.

In a way, this seems like the very brief moment in history in which Europe must choose between a decisive cohesion – and again unearths the cultural, economical and political strategies to become competitive and relevant within a changing world – or again the atomisation into a myriad of proud and diverse nations that, given the ongoing global geo-political rearrangements, have apparently become too small to survive the global 'market'.

Considering that the method of 'scenario thinking', as invented by Hollywood-inspired military intelligence, is still the best way to think about the future, the options that Europe is facing at the present moment would already give us two important scenarios on which to consider 'the future of European architecture'.

The first option, ultimately that of the United States of Europe, is undoubtedly the optimistic scenario. This is the scenario in which most Europeans of younger generations potentially believe, even if they bluntly fail to express their views, in the midst of a mélange of hopelessness, anomie and predictable escapism. Within this scenario, if a strong leadership would rise to the challenge, the problems of the European Union would eventually be overcome by the sheer financial wealth, cultural capital, technical capacity and general creativity of the circa 730 million residents of the continent, as defined in its traditional geographical boundaries.

Beyond Olympic gold medals accounting – which puts Europe far ahead of any other comparable world region – one could hypothesise that, in such a context, the production of high quality architecture is indeed a good index of Europe's potential for the future.

The specific way in which Europe educates and produces architects, the way it welcomes innovative and socially responsible architecture, the way it takes care of its cities and public spaces, how it manages to export the professional and creative knowledge that arises from the field of architecture, could potentially offer an example for how Europe can overcome its current problems in a sustainable way.

Looking into these possibilities in non-scientific fashion, my first idea was to ask the editor of *ArchDaily* how did European architecture fare in the pages of the most viewed architecture website in the world during the year of all crises. The answer came swift, and it confirmed my intuition. Out of 4,909 architectural projects published in *ArchDaily* during 2012, 2,330 were produced within European countries. Even if, at its 740 million inhabitants, the European continent represents only about 11% of the world's population, European architects accomplished at least 47% of the published architecture on a reliable global index of architectural production. And this excludes all the projects that were produced by European architects in other continents – a number that I was not provided but that, given the European 'crisis', I suspect would also be pretty high.

These numbers suggest that, given its prioritisation of democratic access to education and culture, and even amidst its crises, Europe has been pretty successful in producing – and exporting – a valued cultural and economic asset such as that of architecture. Of course, this value was directly associated to a construction market that would itself prove to be a mirage and an unrealistic measure of Europe's capacity for growth. But, on the other hand, it also offered an indication of a capacity to innovate and generate models ready to be emulated by many beyond its frontiers. Beyond solid export values, the abundant and qualified production of European architecture has consistently attested the potential of Europe's core values. If only the investment in these values would remain in place – rather than being replaced by the savage disinvestment on education, culture, and the very employment of a whole generation that benefited from those same high standards – perhaps Europe could endure through the economical storms ahead.

Nonetheless, the mere possibility of continuing such an investment is itself only a part of the optimistic scenario in which Europe reunites around a common political project and manages to overcome its current problems through a continued reinvention – and effective use – of its population's cultural, scientific and entrepreneuring capacities. In the *other* scenario – the scenario in which Europe drops its common goals and ambitions, and fells prey to overspread Balkanisation – this investment would be left to individual nations. And here we may start dwelling into darker predictions. Left on their own, European nations may enter a survival mode determined by the dwindling dimension of their own consumer markets and the new difficulties of trading internationally. As it is already happening in the context of a still lingering European Union, they would surely be even less able to invest in the aforementioned values of education, as in those of cultural and scientific production – like that of high-quality architecture. Beyond any ideological choice, the possibility of maintaining such investments was largely a surplus product of a prosperity typically related to the mirage of consumption and the growth of aspiring middle-classes after World War II. When, instead, nations see themselves propelled by economical forces to destroy those same middle-classes, they loose both the potential of prosperity and reinvention that seems to be the characteristic of that social group. In the scenario of national atomisation that follows, also European architecture would be quickly led to go 'back to basics'. Inevitably reduced to the most constrained and meagre aspects of 'providing shelter', it would tend to loose its competitive edge as an export asset.

Considering that, in the possibility of a regression to such a scenario, the current crisis of Southern European countries can be deemed a true *avant-garde,* it may be useful to look at the nation that has hosted the Prize for the last twenty-five years. Returning to the *ArchDaily* data I've quoted earlier, during 2012 architects from Spain have published 391 projects intended for, or actually built, in their own country. This accounts for about 17% of the total publications by European architects in *ArchDaily,* which is not bad for a country that in terms of population represents about 6% of Europe's total. If we admit that the publication of architectural projects correlates to some degree of perceived quality by peers, it is also interesting to mention that this number represents a potentially high-quality architectural production of 8.2 projects per million inhabitants, when the same ratio was of 1.7 for Germany, 2.8 for the United States, or, most blatantly, 0.2 for China.

We can concede that, from an economical point of view, Spain benefited enormously from its integration in Europe. We can also admit that its architectural boom was correlated to a dangerous bubble in the country's construction sector. Once that bubble burst, its architectural production came tumbling down to almost zero, suggesting that its high level of architecture publications around 2012 was, in itself, a swan's song of an unsustainable progression. What we however also have to take into consideration is that Spain's architectural wealth is still *there.* Even if temporarily dormant or undergoing convulsions, its architects still represent an enormous potential in terms of the export of design intelligence.

The appreciation of this potential is then twofold, and again encroaches with the two scenarios described earlier. If we anticipate a common European strategy for its own cultural and economical development, this design intelligence will find a way to redistribute itself through a wider network of demand, both inside and beyond Europe's frontiers. If, on the other hand, we see Europe atomising back to the level of its individual States and individual initiative, a great part of that design intelligence will stagnate – as, in the midst of the crisis, it is already the case – and eventually asphyxiate. In a fierce Darwinist twist, only the fittest – not necessarily the biggest, or the average – will survive and the great majority of Spain's untapped architectural potential will disappear without a trace. Which seems a rather pitiable perspective after so much has been invested in the materialisation of the specific cultural value that is today embodied in European architecture.

Nevertheless, the two scenarios briefly described here – as some of the possible effects they can have in the future of European architecture – are still missing the impact of some relevant aspects of the current European crisis, which obviously tend to aggravate and complicate the issues involved in this rather intuitive analysis.

In considering the future of architectural practice in Europe we must bring other contextual elements into the equation, namely some questions that hit the front pages of newspapers a little less frequently. Europe is ageing. Its population is gradually shrinking. Younger generations are forced to flee elsewhere with their cultural capital and economical potential. If Europe's middle classes are to be slowly crushed by unemployment and decreasing resources, inequality will grow. The welfare state and its promise of prosperity will crumble. While other regions become economically more attractive, an impoverished Europe will loose its appeal to immigrant populations. In historical terms, this could represent the inevitable moment of the continent's decline. A decline that would only be faster in the case of Europe's inability to construct a common project, with its consequent downward slide into atomisation.

Beyond the scenarios depicted here, though, how can we see these particular aspects translating into the future of European architecture? Naturally, and while Europe's political leaders remain undecided on what choices they must make for its future, architects, as other social groups, have already started to internalise the impact of these broader changes. As professional agents – and also as informed citizens of this abstract, unconcluded project – architects, as their clients and commissioners, have already started to unconsciously accommodate and enact the possibilities and conditionalities of these historical modifications.

Architectural programmes are already being fine-tuned for the needs of an older or unoccupied population. While the remainders of the real-estate boom persist uninhabited, new construction is already being substituted by reconstruction, rehabilitation and renovation. And as energetic and material resources diminish, new building technologies are to be developed so as to guarantee alternative solutions to an hyper-regulated, and much too expensive construction industry.

In addition to all this, other changes in the nature of architectural practice also reveal how European architects may well prove to be extremely adaptive, particularly when they are in possession of a highly prized cultural and creative capital. On a different note, a strongly educated generation of young architects offers the signs that the profession is reviewing its priorities – and its way of practicing and defining the limits of the architectural discipline – as a subtle reaction to the gloomiest aspects of the worst-case scenarios suggested here.

Where the State looses its capacity to deliver assistance, collaborative and networked practices provide for new inspiration and support, and the architect becomes an orchestrator of bottom-up community aspirations, rather than a go-between of top-down impositions. Collectives of architects offer a substitute for individual authorship and the previous predominance of the called *starchitect* as a symbol of a period of ultra-liberal growth. Other takes on architecture's creative potential delve into artistic and fictional possibilities, simply offering critical insights of society's *malaises,* thus becoming part of persisting cultural circuits that are quintessential to European identity.

These and other emergent developments reflect very intrinsically the impasses of the current European situation – a situation that, as some put, is the result of a crisis of values, rather than one of financial assets. Moreover, however, they also offer a different, more optimist glimpse of the future of European architecture. They reveal that, independently of the political scenarios Europe will come to choose, and beyond the misconceptions of a much-cherished economical sustainability, European architecture may have already accumulated just enough cultural capital to become endurably resilient.

Pedro Gadanho is the Curator of Contemporary Architecture in the Department of Architecture and Design at the Museum of Modern Art MoMA, New York and was a jury member for the 2013 Prize.

THE EUROPE OF CITIES

VICENTE GUALLART

What are the challenges that architecture in Europe is facing at the beginning of the 21st century?

Europe is going through a period of identity crisis; a time when many of its member states have serious economic and social problems; a time when from globalisation we learn that this crisis does not affect everybody equally. Dozens of countries and several regions in the world are undergoing a process of urbanisation and industrialisation, similar to the one that occurred in Europe decades ago, which allows them to grow economically. Never has so much building taken place throughout the world.

This model is no longer possible in Europe. Here, cities have already been built. We are experiencing a time of urban maturity that must not be confused with one of decadence. Indeed, if such decadence exists at all, it is more cultural and strategic than physical. Europe constituted the setting for the invention of modern architecture, which made it possible to construct buildings and cities throughout the 20th century. Its culminating moment came almost one hundred years ago, during the between-war period, with the emergence of schools such as the Bahuaus that defined many of the paradigms on the basis of which we have been building for one hundred years. It was an environment in which disciplines became mixed, in which art and new industrial technologies stimulated the rise of creators who defined paradigms for the architecture and the city of their own and future generations.

And today, one hundred years later, we are in a similar situation. We witness a changing cultural, technological and social era based on the development of information technologies which, though they have connected the world, on many occasions have disconnected us from reality. The Internet has changed our lives, but it has yet to change our cities. We live in a world of cities. The real economy is produced in cities; people live in cities; energy is consumed in cities. And our cities in Europe are already built. Urbanism, a term coined in Barcelona by the man who planned the city's *Eixample* (extension), Ildefons Cerdà, defined a rational process by which to transform agricultural or natural land into urban territory. It was a process that served to add value to the land situated around the historical urban settlements located inside the walls to offer a new urban habitat to the new citizens attracted to cities during the latter's industrialisation process.

Now, urbanisation as it was understood in the mid-19th century as something on a blank canvas is no longer possible; but neither is it possible as it was developed during the 20th century on the basis of the *tabula rasa* of historical territories. Urbanism as we knew it no longer makes sense, since it is not accompanied by new urban development.

And what is the prospect for our old European cities? Decadence?

A city is alive if value is added to it. And our cities must meet the great challenge of becoming productive once again, of generating the resources they need in order to function. The industrial city subcontracted the generation of the resources it needed from outside, from the surrounding territory, and later from distant countries. In the forthcoming years, cities must generate the resources they need in order to function and become productive once again. Cities must generate all the energy they need from renewable sources and from the distributive management of their resources. The Internet model must be applied to energy in cities. Similarly, water must be recycled and the process of food production reintegrated into the urban environment and its surroundings. Furthermore, industry must go back to the cities in the form of digital production of goods, produced in real time and in a personalised way, so that what we refer to as the 'knowledge city' uses its knowledge to produce things. We must build a new paradigm around the self-sufficient city. The notion that Europe thinks and Asia manufactures will serve only to exacerbate the decline of our economy and of our cities. Consequently, over the forthcoming years they must be endowed with a metabolism that will allow them to interiorise the generation and internal management of the necessary resources. Today's cities are defined by a kind of urbanism that has ceased to be strategic to become purely tactical, and in most cases by technical processes guided by economic logic. Buildings are defined by their form and function, but now they must also be defined by their metabolism, by their capacity to produce and manage the goods flows that allow them to function.

And herein lies the great opportunity for architecture. If modern architecture was a '*machine à habiter*' and was built from steel, concrete and glass, advanced architecture must be more of an 'organism to create': buildings in which we live, work or rest that make a micro-city out of each place we inhabit; buildings created from the new materials and processes of our times; buildings in which people are no longer merely inhabitants and consumers of resources from outside but net creators of wealth for themselves and for their surroundings. Instead of adhering to the centralised models of industrial architecture, we may now adopt the distributed systems characteristic of information technology. Globalisation, which allows information to flow all over the world, must serve to make architecture connect us to specific sites in each city, in every place on the territory. Architecture connects us to the districts and streets of every city. The sense of community is what makes the city a city. Cities, as a physical structure, are a miracle, produced as fruit of a pact of coexistence.

Architecture must be at the service of the city. Every constructed system has a regular built basis and iconic elements that stand out against the urban tissue.

If much of modern architecture was devoted to defining rules and systems for the construction of a new regular paradigm for a new city, we are now faced with the same challenge.

The great modern masters worked to secure the quality of the average building and thus, in the form either of social housing or high-rise office blocks, many of the best buildings of the 20th century were constructed. The decades of permanent tension on the part of cities to build the most striking icon came to an end.

Now, much of the challenge we face involves redefining the very meaning of the building, from which we must ask more: buildings as organisms that produce the resources they need and relate to their neighbours as if in a network woven from the exchange of social and environmental relations. Many of the new principles of smarter, more ecological architecture are in the process of being adopted by contemporary architectural culture so that it may build urban tissues and icons of architecture that will define the culture of our times. If modern architecture taught us that form follows function, advanced architecture proposes that form follows energy. Buildings, like any construction of nature, attain excellence when on observing, visiting or using them we become aware of what they are and what they do.

We are facing a further challenge. Architecture as a whole will no longer be *ex-novo*; rather, much of our work will involve not rehabilitating but recycling urban material built in past decades. A high percentage of European urban material built after World War II requires regeneration in order to meet the performative standards we expect in which to live. Thus, we must invest part of our energies in recycling districts through the introduction of new urban functions that transform them into productive environments (in terms of the economy and social interaction) and transforming buildings so that they attain maximum functionality with just the right amount of investment.

The reinvention of Europe must begin in its cities and its buildings. If new values exist for Old Europe, they are based on innovation and on transformation of its urban tissue in order to foster a new, more productive and cohesive way of life.

The moment has come for the most radical innovation in architecture.

Vicente Guallart is the Chief Architect for the Barcelona City Hall.

Constructing Europe

Timeline
1988_2013

This timeline contextualises the Prize in terms of some of the major events that have happened during the last twenty-five years.

25 Years
of Architecture

European Union Prize
for Contemporary Architecture
Mies van der Rohe Award

Borges & Irmão Bank
Vila do Conde, Portugal
Álvaro Siza Vieira

New Terminal Development Stansted Airport
London, United Kingdom
Norman Foster/Norman Foster + Partners

1988

1990

—8.000

—4.000

—2.000

—1.000

1988

1990

1989

eurostock

—500

1988
Science
Transatlantic optical fiber telephone
cable enters service.
A Brief History of Time by Stephen
Hawking is published.

Culture
MoMA exhibition, *Deconstructivist
Architecture* opens.
The first major computer virus infects
computers connected to the Internet.

Politics
National strikes in Poland.

Architecture
Pritzker Prize awarded to Gordon
Bunshaft (USA) and Oscar Niemeyer
(Brazil).

1989
Science
World Wide Web created by Tim
Berners-Lee.
Exxon Valdez oil spill.

Culture
I.M. Pei's addition to the Louvre in Paris
opens.
Salvador Dalí dies in Figueres.

Politics
Steel Curtain falls, thus creating an
opportunity to unify Europe.
Mikhail Gorbachev is named President
of the Soviet Union.
Soldarity gains overwhelming victory in
Polish elections.
East German government resigns and
Berlin Wall is demolished.
'Velvet Revolution' in Czechoslovakia
and Václav Havel becomes President.
Nicolae Ceauşescu is overthrown and
executed in Romania.
End of Soviet invasion of Afghanistan.
Thousands of students killed on
Tiananmen Square in Beijing.
Austria formally requests to join the
European Community.

Architecture
Pritzker Prize awarded to Frank Gehry (USA).

1990
Science
80 nations agree to stop producing
ozone layer damaging CFCs by the
year 2000.
The Internet goes public.

Politics
Reunification of Germany and Helmut
Kohl elected Chancellor.
After 27 years behind bars Nelson
Mandela is freed.
End of Augusto Pinochet military
dictatorship in Chile.

Architecture
Pritzker Prize awarded to Aldo Rossi (Italy).
UIA Gold Medal to Charles Correa (India).

1991
Politics
Dissolution of the Soviet Union and
independence of 15 former Soviet
republics. Boris Yeltsin becomes the first
President of the Russian Federation.
Suicide bomber kills former India prime

Kunsthaus Bregenz
Bregenz, Austria
Peter Zumthor

1998

Kursaal Congress Centre and Auditorium
San Sebastián, Spain
Rafael Moneo

2001

Emerging Architect Special Mention:
Kaufmann Holz Distribution Centre
Bobingen, Germany
Florian Nagler/Nagler Architekten

8.000

4.000

2.000

Google

1998

2001

1.000

1997

1998

1999

2000

2002

500

Culture
Diana, Princess of Wales, is killed in a car accident in Paris.
Guggenheim Museum Bilbao designed by Frank Gehry opens.

Politics
Signing of the Treaty of Amsterdam, which aims to reform the EU institutions. EU leaders agree to start the process of membership negotiations with 10 countries of central and Eastern Europe: Bulgaria, the Czech Republic, Estonia, Hungary, Latvia, Lithuania, Poland, Romania, Slovakia and Slovenia. The Mediterranean islands of Cyprus and Malta are also included.

Architecture
Pritzker Prize awarded to Sverre Fehn (Norway).

1998
Science
Explosive growth of the Internet. E-mail becomes popular.

Politics
India and Pakistan conduct first nuclear tests. Peace accord in Northern Ireland. President Clinton impeached by Republicans on Capitol Hill.

Culture
Lisbon World Exposition Expo'98.

Architecture
Pritzker Prize awarded to Renzo Piano (Italy).

1999
Science
Irruption of Hot Pot and Moodle. World population reaches 6 billion.

Politics
The euro is introduced in 11 countries (joined by Greece in 2001) for commercial and financial transactions only. The euro countries are Belgium, Germany, Greece, Spain, France, Ireland, Italy, Luxembourg, The Netherlands, Austria, Portugal and

Finland. Denmark, Sweden and the United Kingdom decide to stay out for the time being.
Hugo Chavez becomes President of Venezuela.

Architecture
Pritzker Prize awarded to Norman Foster (United Kingdom)
The UIA Gold Medal to Ricardo Legorreta (Mexico).

2000
Science
DNA sequencing of human genome roughly completed.
Sharp decline of NASDAQ and of dot.com businesses.
International Space Station begins operations.

Politics
George W. Bush is elected President of the United States.
Vladimir Putin becomes President of Russia.

Global Warming Conference at The Hague fails.

Culture
Tate Modern in London opens.

Architecture
Pritzker Prize awarded to Rem Koolhaas (The Netherlands).
7th Venice Architecture Biennale, directed by Massimiliano Fuksas, titled: *Less Aesthetics, More Ethics.*

2001
Science
US National Academy of Science predicts global temperature rise 2.5 to 10 degrees Fahrenheit by the end of the century.

Culture
Talibans blow up Buddha statues in Afghanistan.
Wikipedia founded.
Launch of the iPod.

Politics
11 September becomes synonymous with the 'War on Terror' after hijacked airliners are flown into buildings in New York and Washington.
Signing of Nice Treaty, implementing reforms of European institutions and reinforcing fundamental rights, security and defense, and judicial cooperation in criminal.
Silvio Berlusconi's rightwing coalition wins in Italy.
Rioting related to economic crisis causes change of government in Argentina.

Architecture
Pritzker Prize awarded to Jaques Herzog & Pierre de Meuron (Switzerland).

2002
Science
The appearance of Google makes it unnecessary to pass round collections of 'useful web links'.
2-mile thick pollution cloud over South Asia causing death of half-million people annually.

Politics
Leftist Lula da Silva wins election in Brazil.
Euro notes and coins arrive. Printing, minting and distributing them in 12 countries is a major logistical operation.

Architecture
Pritzker Prize awarded to Glenn Murcutt (Australia).
The UIA Gold Medal to Renzo Piano (Italy).
8th Venice Architecture Biennale, directed by Deyan Sudjic, titled: *Next.*

Car Park and Terminus Hoenheim North
Strasbourg, France
Zaha Hadid/Zaha Hadid Architects

Emerging Architect Special Mention:
Scharnhauser Park Town Hall
Ostfildern, Germany
J. Mayer H.

Netherlands Embassy
Berlin, Germany
OMA/Rem Koolhaas, Ellen van Loon

Emerging Architect Especial Mention:
BasketBar
Utrecht, The Netherlands
**Pieter Bannenberg, Walter van
Dijk, Kamiel Klaasse, Mark
Linnemann/NL Architects**

MUSAC Contemporary Art Museum of Castilla y León
León, Spain
Luis M. Mansilla, Emilio Tuñón/Mansilla + Tuñón Arquitectos

Emerging Architect Especial Mention:
Faculty of Mathematics
Ljubljana, Slovenia
**Matija Bevk, Vasa J. Perović
Bevk Perović Arhitekti**

2003 • 2004 • 2005 • 2006 • 2007 • 2008

2003
Science
The Human Genome Project is completed.

Politics
North Korea abandons Nuclear Non-proliferation treaty.
US-led troops invade and occupy Iraq.
As part of its foreign and security policy, the EU takes on peace-keeping operations in the Balkans, firstly in the Former Yugoslav Republic of Macedonia, and then in Bosnia and Herzegovina.

Architecture
The Pritzker Prize awarded to Jørn Utzon (Denmark).

2004
Science
Major tsunami disaster around the Indian Ocean. Over 150,000 people perish.

Politics
Terrorists kill 190 people in Madrid train bombings. Government defeated in subsequent election.
The PSOE wins the elections in Spain and José Luis Rodriguez Zapatero becomes President of Spain.
Conservatives sweep elections in US. George W. Bush re-elected President.
Eight countries of central and Eastern Europe — the Czech Republic, Estonia, Latvia, Lithuania, Hungary, Poland, Slovenia and Slovakia — join the EU, finally ending the division of Europe decided by the Great Powers 60 years earlier at Yalta. Cyprus and Malta also become members.
The 25 EU countries sign a Treaty establishing a European Constitution.

Architecture
Pritzker Prize awarded to Zaha Hadid (United Kingdom).
9th Venice Architecture Biennale, directed by Kurt W. Forster, titled: *Metamorph.*

2005
Science
Large numbers of users become aware of 'web 2.0 technologies'.
Hurricane Katrina destroys New Orleans.
150 nations agree to launch talks on mandatory post-2012 reductions in greenhouse gases, talks that will exclude an unwilling US.

Politics
Mahmoud Ahmadinejad becomes President of Iran.
Angela Merkel elected: first female Chancellor of Germany.
France and The Netherlands reject the Constitution of the European Union.

Architecture
Pritzker Prize awarded to Tom Mayne (USA).
The UIA Gold Medal to Tadao Ando (Japan).

2006
Science
NASA report: Arctic Sea ice is melting 9% a decade.
The communications revolution continues. Many schools and homes now have high-speed access to the Internet.

Politics
Ellen Johnson Sirleaf becomes President of Liberia, and thus Africa's first elected female head of state.

Architecture
Pritzker Prize awarded to Paulo Mendes da Rocha (Brazil).
10th Venice Architecture Biennale directed by Ricky Burdett, titled: *Cities, Architecture and Societies.*

2007
Science
The iPhone launched by Steve Jobs.
Intergovernmental Panel on Climate Change IPCC concludes that human caused change was unequivocal.
US sub-prime woes lead to housing market crash and credit crisis worldwide.

Politics
Nicolas Sarkozy wins French presidential election.
Gordon Brown succeeds Tony Blair as British PM.
Two more countries from Eastern Europe, Bulgaria and Romania, now join the EU, bringing the number of member states to 27 countries.
The 27 EU countries sign the Treaty of Lisbon, which amends the previous Treaties.

Architecture
Pritzker Prize awarded to Richard Rogers (United Kingdom).

2008
Science
Widespread use of mobile phone. The spread of broadband allows for Skype video conferencing, podcasting and YouTube reaching millions of people.
Facebook becomes popular (created in 2004). Twitter becomes popular (created in 2006).
Financial meltdown of American banks spreads to Europe and Asia. Governments inject enormous amounts of bailout money to deal with a global credit crises.

Culture
'Water Cube, 'Bird's Nest', South Railway Station, and other buildings in Beijing, completed for the Summer Olympics.

Politics
Barack Obama elected President of the USA.
A financial crisis hits the global economy in September 2008, leading to closer economic cooperation between EU countries.

Municipal Sports Stadium
Badalona, Spain
Esteve Bonell, Francesc Rius

1992

Waterloo International Station
London, United Kingdom
Nicholas Grimshaw/Nicholas Grimshaw & Partners

1994

French National Library
Paris, France
Dominique Perrault/Dominique Perrault Architecture

1996

1991 — 1992 — 1993 — 1994 — 1995 — 1996

---

minister Rajiv Gandhi.
South African President F. W. de Klerk announces abolition of apartheid laws. In the Balkans, Yugoslavia begins to break down. Fighting starts first in Croatia, then in Bosnia and Herzegovina where Serbs, Croats and Muslims fight in a bloody civil war.

Architecture
Pritzker Prize awarded to Robert Venturi (USA).
5th Venice Architecture Biennale, directed by Francesco Dal Co.

1992
Science
Earth summit held in Rio. Convention on Protection of Species and Habitat signed.

Culture
Summer Olympic Games held in Barcelona.

Politics
Maastricht Treaty creates the European

Union: monetary union by 1999, new common policy, European citizenship, security policy, and improved internal security.
Bill Clinton wins presidency in USA. NAFTA Trade Pact signed by USA, Canada and Mexico.
Serbia and Montenegro proclaimed a new Federal Republic of Yugoslavia.

Architecture
Pritzker Prize awarded to Álvaro Siza (Portugal).

1993
Science
First web browser, Netscape, created by Marc Andreessen.

Politics
The European single market and its four freedoms are established: the free movement of goods, services, people and money is now a reality. More than 200 laws have been agreed since 1986 covering tax policy, business regula-

tions, professional qualifications, etc. to open frontiers.
The Copenhagen criteria is determined: the rules that define whether a country is eligible to join the European Union. Slovakia and Czech Republic peacefully split.
Oslo I Accord ends First Intifada between Israel and Palestine.

Architecture
Pritzker Prize and the UIA Gold Medal awarded to Fumihiko Maki (Japan).

1994
Science
Opening of the Channel Tunnel.

Culture
Chauvet cave discovered in France, with paintings more than 30,000 years old. Death of Kurt Cobain.

Politics
IRA ceasefire lifts hope for peace in Ireland.

Nelson Mandela sworn in as President of South Africa.
Rwandan Genocide: 1 million Tutsis are killed by Hutus.

Architecture
Pritzker Prize awarded to Christian de Portzamparc (France).

1995
Science
Earthquake hits Kobe, Japan.
Bank scandal in London: Barings Bank faces insolvency.
Panic in Osaka: Collapse of largest credit union in Japan.

Politics
Jacques Chirac elected President of France.
The leaders of Serbia, Bosnia, and Croatia sign a peace agreement in Dayton, Ohio. Israeli Prime Minister Isaac Rabin assassinated in Jerusalem.
Establishment of the World Trade Organization.

Austria, Finland and Sweden join the EU, bringing its membership to 15. Norway stays out again following a referendum in which a majority of people voted against membership. The Schengen Agreement takes effect in seven countries — Belgium, Germany, Spain, France, Luxembourg, The Netherlands and Portugal. Citizens of any of these nationalities are allowed to travel between all these countries without any passport control at the frontiers.

Architecture
Pritzker Prize awarded to Tadao Ando (Japan).

1996
Science
Scottish researcher creates clone lamb from adult sheep DNA.
Avatar based multiuse worlds developed.
Rapid adoption of Internet.

Politics
Benjamin Netanyahu, of the Likud party, wins the Israeli elections. Talibans conquer Afghanistan. Millions of young people study in other countries with EU support.

Architecture
Pritzker Prize and the UIA Gold Medal awarded to Rafael Moneo (Spain).
6th Venice Architecture Biennale, directed by Hans Hollein, titled: *Sensing the Future—The Architect as Seismograph.*
The International Union of Architects Congress held in Barcelona: *Present and Futures. Architecture in Cities.*

1997
Science
Kyoto Protocol Convention on Climate Change.
Beginning of Asian economic crises after Japan raises its national consumption tax and Thailand lets its currency float.

Norwegian National Opera & Ballet
Oslo, Norway
SNØHETTA/Kjetil Trædal Thorsen, Tarald Lundevall, Craig Dykers

2009

Emerging Architect Special Mention:
Gymnasium 46° 09'N/16° 50'E
Koprivnica, Croatia
Lea Pelivan, Toma Plejić/STUDIO UP

Neues Museum
Berlin, Germany
David Chipperfield Architects in collaboration with Julian Harrap

2011

Emerging Architect Special Mention:
Collage House
Girona, Spain
Ramon Bosch, Bet Capdeferro
bosch.capdeferro arquitectures

Harpa Reykjavik Concert Hall and Conference Centre. Reykjavik, Iceland
Peer Teglgaard Jeppesen, Osbjørn Jacobsen/Henning Larsen Architects
Olafur Eliasson/Studio Olafur Eliasson Sigurður Einarsson/Batteríið Architects

2013

Emerging Architect Especial Mention:
Red Bull Music Academy
Madrid, Spain
María Langarita, Víctor Navarro
Langarita-Navarro Arquitectos

8.000

4.000

2009   2010   2011   2012   2013

2.000

1.000

500

Architecture
Pritzker Prize awarded to Jean Nouvel (France).
The UIA Gold Medal to Teodoro González de León (Mexico).
11th Venice Architecture Biennale: directed by Aaron Betsky, titled: *Out There: Architecture Beyond Building.*

2009
Science
UN climate conference in Copenhagen fails to agree on a binding deal to reduce CO2 emissions. It narrowly escapes collapse by agreeing to recognise a political accord brokered by Obama with China & other emerging powers.

Culture
Death of Michael Jackson.

Politics
Formation of BRICS economic bloc.
The Treaty of Lisbon is ratified by all EU countries before entering into

force on 1 December. It provides the EU with modern institutions and more efficient working methods.

Architecture
Pritzker Prize awarded to Peter Zumthor (Switzerland).

2010
Science
Major earthquake in Haiti, over 200,000 people perish. International rescue help pours into Haiti.

Culture
The website Wikileaks releases thousands of classified US documents.

Politics
Threat of Greece defaulting on its debts triggers the European sovereign debt crisis and Ireland's bankruptcy.
Eurozone in crisis.
David Cameron becomes Prime Minister of the United Kingdom.

Dilma Rousseff becomes first female president in Brazil.

Architecture
Pritzker Prize awarded to Kazuyo Sejima and Ryue Nishizawa (Japan).
Burj Khalifa by SOM, the tallest skyscraper in the world, is completed.
12th Venice Architecture Biennale, directed by Kazuyo Sejima, titled: *People Meet in Architecture.*

2011
Science
A 9.0 earthquake near Tohoku, Japan, triggers a tsunami that results in 16,000 deaths and the meltdown of the Fukushima Nuclear Power Plant.
Severe debt crisis in Greece, Portugal, Spain and Italy leads to major problems for the entire Eurozone.
Death of Steve Jobs.

Culture
Facebook has more than 600 million active users.

Politics
Arab Spring: revolutions in Tunisia, Egypt and Libya follow, as well as uprisings in Yemen, Syria and Bahrain, and protests in several other Arab countries.
Occupy Wall Street movement spreads from New York to 70 major US cities and to 900 cities worldwide.
Afghan war becomes the longest war in US history. Barack Obama announces troop withdrawals from 2012 to 2014.
Deaths of Muammar Gaddafi, Osama bin Laden and Kim Jong Il.
Iraq War ends.
World population reaches 7 billion.

Architecture
Pritzker Prize awarded to Eduardo Souto de Moura (Portugal).
The UIA Gold Medal to Álvaro Siza (Portugal).

2012
Science
Skydiver Felix Baumgartner becomes the first person to break the sound barrier without a vehicle

Culture
The Chinese novelist Mo Yan wins the Nobel Prize in literature.

Architecture
Pritzker Prize awarded to Wang Shu (China).
13th Venice Architecture Biennale: directed by David Chipperfield, titled: *Common Ground.*
Oscar Niemeyer dies.

2013
Science
Canada becomes the first country to withdraw from the United Nations Convention to Combat Desertification.

CO2 level exceeds 400 parts per million.
Scientists clone human stem cells.

Politics
The European Union agree to €10 billion bailout for Cyprus.
The United Nations General Assembly adopts the Arms Trade Treaty to regulate the international trade of conventional weapons.
An eight-story commercial building collapses in Savar Upazila near the Bangladeshi capital Dhaka, resulting in at least 675 dead.
Hugo Chavez dies: Nicolás Maduro elected President of Venezuela.
Death of Margaret Thatcher.

Architecture
Pritzker Prize awarded to Toyo Ito (Japan).

The Authors

Kenneth Frampton

Kenneth Frampton is the Ware Professor of Architecture at Columbia University in New York. He was the Chair of the jury for the 1988 and 1990 awards.

Vittorio Gregotti

Vittorio Gregotti, a principal of Gregotti Associati in Milan and professor at the Università Iuav di Venezia, was a member of the jury for the 1988 and 1990 editions of the Prize.

Ignasi de Solà-Morales

A professor at the Escola Tècnica Superior d'Arquitectura de Barcelona, Ignasi de Solà-Morales (1942-2001) was a jury member for the first four editions of the Prize.

Vittorio Magnago Lampugnani

Vittorio Magnago Lampugnani is a professor at the ETH Zurich. He was the Chair for the 1998 and 2001 juries and the Director of the Deutsches Architekturmuseum DAM when the exhibition *European Architecture 1984-1994* was presented there.

Dietmar Steiner

Dietmar Steiner has been the Director of the Architekturzentrum Wien AzW since it opened in 1993. He was a member of the jury from 1996 to 2001 and then again in 2007.

Elia Zenghelis

Elia Zenghelis has taught at numerous institutions such as the Kunstakademie in Düsseldorf and the Berlage Institute in Rotterdam. He was a member of the award jury from 1994-2001.

Aaron Betsky

Director of the Cincinnati Art Museum since 2006, Aaron Betsky is the former Director of the Nederlands Architectuurinstituut NAi, Rotterdam. He was a jury member in 2003 and 2005.

Mohsen Mostafavi

Mohsen Mostafavi is the Dean of the Harvard Graduate School of Design and the Alexander and Victoria Wiley Professor of Design. He was a jury member for the 2005 award and he chaired the jury in 2011.

Ricky Burdett

Ricky Burdett is professor of urban studies at the London School of Economics and Political Science LSE and Director of LSE Cities and the Urban Age programme. He was the Chair of the jury for the 2007 award.

Luis Fernández-Galiano

A professor at the Escuela Técnica Superior de Arquitectura de Madrid, Luis Fernández-Galiano is the editor of *AV Monografías* and *Arquitectura Viva*. He was a jury member for the 2007 award when the MUSAC by Luis M. Mansilla (1959-2012) and Emilio Tuñón received the Prize.

Peter Cachola Schmal

Peter Cachola Schmal is the Director at the Deutsches Architekturmuseum DAM in Frankfurt since 2006. He was on the jury of the 2007 Prize.

Francis Rambert

Francis Rambert is the Director of the Institut français d'architecture Ifa, Cité de l'architecture & du patrimoine since 2003. He was a jury member for the 2005 and 2007 award editions and he chaired the jury in 2009.

Ole Bouman

Ole Bouman, Creative Director of the Shenzhen Biennale, is the former Director of the Nederlands Architectuurinstituut NAi and he formed part of the jury for the 2009 and 2011 editions.

Fulvio Irace

A professor at the Politecnico di Milano, Fulvio Irace is the former architecture curator of the Triennale di Milano. He was a member of the 2009 award jury.

Ewa P. Porębska

Ewa P. Porębska is the editor-in-chief of *Architektura-murator* and was a jury member for the 2013 Prize.

Kent Martinussen

Kent Martinussen is the CEO of the Danish Architecture Center and formed part of the 2013 jury.

Hans Ibelings

Hans Ibelings was the co-founder and editor-in-chief of the magazine *A10* and has recently launched *The Architecture Observer*.

Pau de Solà-Morales

Pau de Solà-Morales is a professor at the Escola Tècnica Superior d'Arquitectura de Reus.

Sarah Mineko Ichioka

Sarah Mineko Ichioka is the Director of the Architecture Foundation in London and the Co-Director of the London Festival of Architecture.

Pedro Gadanho

Pedro Gadanho is the Curator of Contemporary Architecture in the Department of Architecture and Design at the Museum of Modern Art MoMA, New York and was a jury member for the 2013 Prize.

Vicente Guallart

Vicente Guallart is the Chief Architect for the Barcelona City Hall.

The Works

Prize Winner 1994

Waterloo International Station
London, United Kingdom
Nicholas Grimshaw/Nicholas Grimshaw & Partners
www.grimshaw-architects.com
Client: British Railways Board – European Passenger Services Ltd

Shortlisted 1994

Postmen's Flats
Paris, France
Philippe Gazeau
Philippe Gazeau Architecte
www.philippegazeau.com
Client: SA HLM Toit et Joie

Shortlisted 1994

Maastricht Academy of Arts and Architecture
Maastricht, The Netherlands
Wiel Arets/Wiel Arets Architects
www.wielaretsarchitects.nl
Client: Rijkschogeschool Maastricht

Shortlisted 1994

L'Illa Diagonal Block
Barcelona, Spain
Rafael Moneo, Manuel de Solà-Morales
Client: Winterthur

Prize Winner 1996

French National Library
Paris, France
Dominique Perrault
Dominique Perrault Architecture
www.perraultarchitecture.com
Client: Ministry of Culture of France

Finalist 1996

European Archaeological Centre of Mont Beuvray
Mont Beuvray, France
Pierre-Louis Faloci
www.pierrelouisfaloci.com
Client: SEM du Mont Beuvray
Ministère de la culture

Finalist 1996

Aukrust Centre
Alvdal, Norway
Sverre Fehn/Sverre Fehn Architect
Client: Aukrustsenteret A/S v/Alvdal Kommune og Aukruststiftelsen

Finalist: 1996

Thermal Bath
Vals, Switzerland
Peter Zumthor
Büro Peter Zumthor
Client: Community of Vals

Prize Winner 1998

Kunsthaus Bregenz
Bregenz, Austria
Peter Zumthor
Büro Peter Zumthor
Client: Vorarlberger Landesregierung

Finalist 1998

Museum Liner Appenzell
Appenzell, Switzerland
Annette Gigon, Mike Guyer
A. Gigon/M. Guyer Architekten
www.gigon-guyer.ch
Client: Stiftung Museum Carl Liner Vater und Sohn

Finalist 1998

Jewish Museum
Berlin, Germany
Daniel Libeskind/Studio Daniel Libeskind
Client: Stiftung Juedisches Museum Berlin
www.daniel-libeskind.com
Client: Land Berlin

Finalist 1998

Villa in Bordeaux
Bordeaux, France
Rem Koolhaas, Maarten van Seeveren
OMA
www.oma.com
Client: Private

Finalist 1998

Beyler Foundation Museum
Riehen, Basel, Switzerland
Renzo Piano Building Workshop, architects in association with Burckhardt´+ Partner AG, Basel
www.rpbw.com
Client: Beyeler Foundation Ernst Beyeler, F. Vischer, U. Albrecht (consultants)

Kursaal Congress Centre and
Auditorium
San Sebastián, Spain
Rafael Moneo
Client: Centro Kursaal/Kursaal
Elkargunea

Kaufmann Holz Distribution Centre
Bobingen, Germany
Florian Nagler/Florian Nagler
Architekten
www.nagler-architekten.de
Client: Kaufmann Holz AG.

Altamira Museum & Centre for
Investigation
Santillana del Mar, Cantabria, Spain
Juan Navarro Baldeweg/Navarro
Baldeweg Asociados
www.navarrobaldeweg.net
Client: Consorcio para Altamira
(Ministerio de Cultura, Fundación
Marcelino Botín, Diputación Regional
de Cantabria, Ayuntamiento de
Santillana del Mar, Ministerio de
Economía y Hacienda)

Courthouse
Nantes, France
Jean Nouvel
Architectures Jean Nouvel
www.jeannouvel.com
Client: Ministère de la Justice,
Délégation Générale au Programme
Pluriannuel d'Equipements, France

Nordea Bank
Copenhagen, Denmark
Henning Larsen, Mette Kynne
Frandsen, Louis Becker
Henning Larsen Architects
www.henninglarsen.com
Client: ATP Real Estate

Car Park and Terminus
Hoenheim North
Strasbourg, France
Zaha Hadid
Zaha Hadid Architects
www.zaha-hadid.com
Client: C.U.S (Communaute Urbaine
de Strasbourg)
C.T.S (Compagnie des Transports
Strasbourgeois)

Scharnhauser Park Town Hall
Ostfildern, Germany
Jürgen Mayer H.
www.jmayerh.de
Client: Stadt Ostfildern

Chassé Park Apartments
Breda, The Netherlands
Xaveer De Geyter/Xaveer De Geyter
Architects
www.xdga.be
Client: Chassé CV, joint-venture
Proper Stok Woningen BV and
Wilma Bouw

Palais de Tokyo
Site for Contemporary Creation
Paris, France
Anne Lacaton, Jean-Philippe Vassal
Lacaton & Vassal Architectes
www.lacatonvassal.com
Client: Ministère de la Culture et de la
Communication

Hagen Island
The Hague, The Netherlands
Winy Maas, Jacob van Rijs, Nathalie de
Vries/MVRDV
www.mvrdv.nl
Client: Amvest Vastgoed

Netherlands Embassy Berlin
Berlin, Germany
Rem Koolhaas, Ellen van Loon/OMA
www.oma.com
Client: Netherlands Ministry of Foreign
Affairs – Dienst Gebouwen Buitenland,
La Hague

BasketBar
Utrecht, The Netherlands
Pieter Bannenberg, Walter van Dijk,
Kamiel Klaasse, Mark Linnemann
NL Architects
www.nlarchitects.nl
Client: Universiteit Utrecht Huisvesting,
Aryan Sikkema

30 St Mary Axe (Swiss Re
Headquarters)
London, United Kingdom
Norman Foster /Foster + Partners
www.fosterandpartners.com
Client: Swiss Re

Selfridges & Co Department Store
Birmingham, United Kingdom
Jan Kaplicky, Amanda Levete/Future
Systems
www.future-systems.com
Client: Selfridges & Co

Forum 2004 Esplanade & Photovoltaic
Plant
Barcelona, Spain
José Antonio Martínez Lapeña, Elías
Torres Tur/José Antonio Martínez
Lapeña & Elías Torres Architects
www.jamlet.net
Client: Infraestructures de Llevant,
BIMSA; Ajuntament de Barcelona i
Ajuntament de Sant Adrià del Besòs

Braga Municipal Stadium
Braga, Portugal
Eduardo Souto de Moura
Souto Moura - Arquitectos SA
Client: Braga City Hall

**MUSAC Contemporary Art
Museum of Castilla y León
León, Spain
Luis M. Mansilla, Emilio Tuñón
Mansilla + Tuñón Arquitectos**
www.mansilla-tunon.com
Client: Junta de Castilla y León,
GESTURCAL

Faculty of Mathematics
Ljubljana, Slovenia
Matija Bevk, Vasa J. Perović
Bevk Perović Arhitekti
www.bevkperovic.com
Client: University of Ljubljana

Sines Arts Centre
Sines, Portugal
Francisco Aires Mateus, Manuel Aires
Mateus/Aires Mateus
www.airesmateus.com
Client: Camara Municipal de Sines

Mercedes-Benz Museum
Stuttgart, Germany
Ben van Berkel/UNStudio
www.unstudio.com
Client: DaimlerChrysler Immobilien,
Berlin

America's Cup Building 'Veles e Vents'
Valencia, Spain
David Chipperfield, Fermin Vázquez
David Chipperfield Architects, b720
www.davidchipperfield.com
www.b720.com
Client: Consorcio Valencia 2007

National Choreographic Centre
Aix-en-Provence, France
Rudy Ricciotti /Rudy Ricciotti architecte
www.rudyricciotti.com
Client: Ville d'Aix-en-Provence

Phæno Science Centre
Wolfsburg, Germany
Zaha Hadid/Zaha Hadid Architects
www.zaha-hadid.com
Client: Neulandgesellschaft mbH on
Behalf of the City of Wolfsburg

School of Management
Bordeaux, France
Jean-Philippe Vassal, Anne Lacaton
Lacaton & Vassal Architectes
www.lacatonvassal.com
Client: Ville de Bordeaux

**Norwegian National Opera & Ballet
Oslo, Norway
Kjetil Trædal Thorsen, Tarald
Lundevall, Craig Dykers/SNØHETTA**
www.snohetta.com
Client: Statsbygg - The Governmental
Building Agency

Gymnasium 46° 09' N/16° 50' E
Koprivnica, Croatia
Lea Pelivan, Toma Plejić/Studio Up
www.studioup.hr
Client: Koprivnica Municipal Authority

Library, Senior Citizens' Centre and
Public Space
Barcelona, Spain
Rafael Aranda, Carme Pigem, Ramon
Vilalta/RCR Aranda Pigem Vilalta
Arquitectes
www.rcrarquitectes.es
Client: ProEixample/Ajuntament de
Barcelona

University Luigi Bocconi
Milan, Italy
Shelley McNamara, Yvonne Farrell
Grafton Architects
www.graftonarchitects.ie
Client: Università Luigi Bocconi

Nice Tramway Terminal
Nice, France
Marc Barani/Atelier Marc Barani
www.atelierbarani.com
Client: C.A.N.C.A. Communauté
d'Agglomération Nice Côte d'Azur
Mission Tramway

Zenith Music Hall
Strasbourg, France
Massimiliano Fuksas, Doriana Fuksas
Studio Fuksas
www.fuksas.it
Client: Communauté Urbaine de
Strasbourg

Neues Museum
Berlin, Germany
David Chipperfield
David Chipperfield Architects in
collaboration with Julian Harrap
www.davidchipperfield.com
Client: Stiftung Preußischer Kulturbesitz
represented by Bundesamt für
Bauwesen und Raumordnung

Collage House
Girona, Spain
Ramon Bosch, Bet Capdeferro
bosch.capdeferro arquitectures
www.boschcapdeferro.net
Client: Família Capdeferro

BrOnks Youth Theatre
Brussels, Belgium
Martine De Maeseneer, Dirk Van
den Brande/MDMA Martine De
Maeseneer Architecten
www.mdma.be
Client: VGC Flemish Community
Commission of the Brussels Capital

MAXXI Museum of XXI Century Arts
Rome, Italy
Zaha Hadid, Patrik Schumader
Zaha Hadid Architects
www.zaha-hadid.com
Client: Italian Ministry For Heritage
and Cultural Activities

Danish Radio Concert Hall
Copenhagen, Denmark
Jean Nouvel/Ateliers Jean Nouvel
www.jeannouvel.com
Client: DR: Denmarks Radio, Denmark

Acropolis Museum
Athens, Greece
Bernard Tschumi
Bernard Tschumi Architects
www.tschumi.com
Client: Organization for the Construction
of the New Acropolis Museum

Groot Klimmendaal Rehabilitation
Centre
Arnhem, The Netherlands
Koen van Velsen/Architectenbureau
Koen van Velsen
www.koenvanvelsen.com
Client: Stichting Arnhems
revalidatiecentrum Groot Klimmendaal

Harpa Reykjavik Concert Hall and
Conference Centre
Reykjavik, Iceland
Peer Teglgaard Jeppesen,
Osbjørn Jacobsen
Henning Larsen Architects
www.henninglarsen.com
Olafur Eliasson/Studio Olafur
Eliasson
www.olafureliasson.net
Sigurður Einarsson/Batteríið
architects
www.arkitekt.is
Client: Austurnhofn TR East Harbour
Project

Red Bull Music Academy
Madrid, Spain
María Langarita, Víctor Navarro
Langarita-Navarro Arquitectos
www.langarita-navarro.com
Client: Red Bull España

Market Hall
Ghent, Belgium
Paul Robbrecht, Hilde Daem/Robbrecht
en Daem architecten
www.robbrechtendaem.com
Marie Jose van Hee/Marie-José Van
Hee architecten
www.mjvanhee.be
Client: City of Ghent, VVM De Lijn,
TMVW

Superkilen
Copenhagen, Denmark
Bjarke Ingels, Nanna Gyldholm Møller,
Mikkel Marcker Stubgaard / BIG -
Bjarke Ingels Group
www.big.dk
Jakob Fenger, Rasmus Nielsen,
Bjørnstjerne Christiansen
SUPERFLEX
www.superflex.net
Martin Rein-Cano, Lorenz Dexler
TOPOTEK1
www.topotek1.de
Client: Copenhagen Municipality,
Realdania

Nursing Home
Alcácer do Sal, Portugal
Francisco Aires Mateus, Manuel Aires
Mateus/Aires Mateus
www.airesmateus.com
Client: Santa Casa da Misericordia de
Alcácer do Sal

Metropol Parasol
Seville, Spain
Jürgen Mayer H., Marta Ramírez
Iglesias, André Santer/J. Mayer H.
www.jmayerh.de
Client: Ayuntamiento de Sevilla &
SACYR

The Juries

1988

Kenneth Frampton, Chair
Ricardo Bofill
François Burckhardt
Alessandro Giulianelli
Vittorio Gregotti
Hans Hollein
Ignasi de Solà-Morales, Secretary

1990

Kenneth Frampton, Chair
Ricardo Bofill
François Burkhardt
Vittorio Gregotti
Hans Hollein
Ignasi de Solà-Morales, Secretary

1992

Norman Foster, Chair
Henri E. Ciriani
Kenneth Frampton
Herman Hertzberger
Henning Larsen
Álvaro Siza Vieira
Ignasi de Solà-Morales
Francis Strauven
Elia Zenghelis
Lluís Hortet, Secretary

1994

Norman Foster, Chair
Henri E. Ciriani
Henning Larsen
Fritz Neumeyer
Álvaro Siza Vieira
Ignasi de Solà-Morales
Francis Strauven
Elia Zenghelis
Lluís Hortet, Secretary

1996

Fritz Neumeyer, Chair
Andrej Hrausky
Toyo Ito
Jacques Lucan
Marja-Riitta Norri
Dietmar Steiner
Francesco Venezia
Elia Zenghelis
Lluís Hortet, Secretary

1998

Vittorio M. Lampugnani, Chair
Wiel Arets
Oriol Bohigas
Andrej Hrausky
Marja-Riitta Norri
Dominique Perrault
Dietmar Steiner
Wilfried Wang
Elia Zenghelis
Lluís Hortet, Secretary

2001

Vittorio M. Lampugnani, Chair
Wiel Arets
Esteve Bonell
David Chipperfield
Kristin Feireiss
Luis Fernández-Galiano
Dominique Perrault
Dietmar Steiner
Elia Zenghelis
Lluís Hortet, Secretary

2003

David Chipperfield, Chair
Aaron Betsky
Eduard Bru
Ingeborg Flagge
Shane O'Toole
Matthias Sauerbruch
Kazuyo Sejima
Deyan Sudjic
Alejandro Zaera-Polo
Lluís Hortet, Secretary

2005

Zaha Hadid, Chair
Aaron Betsky
Stefano Boeri (1st meeting)
Eduard Bru
Roberto Collovà
Mohsen Mostafavi
Suha Özkan
Francis Rambert
Kazuyo Sejima
Lluís Hortet, Secretary

2007

Ricky Burdett, Chair
Peter Cachola Schmal
Luís Fernández-Galiano
Beth Galí
Bettina Götz
Ellen van Loon
Mohsen Mostafavi
Francis Rambert
Dietmar Steiner
Lluís Hortet, Secretary

2009

Francis Rambert, Chair
Ole Bouman
Irena Fialová
Fulvio Irace
Luis M. Mansilla
Vasa J. Perović
Carme Pinós
Lluis Hortet, Secretary

2011

Mohsen Mostafavi, Chair
Ole Bouman
Yvonne Farell
Annette Gigon
Anne Lacaton
Tarald Lundevall
Zhu Pei
Lluís Hortet, Secretary

2013

Wiel Arets, Chair
Pedro Gadanho
Antón García Abril
Louisa Hutton
Kent Martinussen
Frédéric Migayrou
Ewa Porębska
Giovanna Carnevali, Secretary

Christina Gräwe
Ulf Grønvold
Vittorio Gregotti
Rob Gregory
Pétur H. Ármannsson
Henrieta H. Moravcíková
Hans Haagensen
Karin Hallas
Alena Hanzlova
Harri Hautajärvi
Gonzalo Herrero Delicado
Anna Hesse
Hans Hollein
Milan Hon
Andrej Hrausky
Špela Hudnik
Hans Ibelings
Fulvio Irace
Anne Isopp
Krunoslav Ivanišin
Wolfgang Jean Stock
Ulrike Jehle-Schulte
Zbigniew K. Zuziak
Luzlim Kabashi
Gabriele Kaiser
Ömer Kanipak
Audrys Karalius
Otto Kapfinger
Gökhan Karakus
Martin Keiding
Ursula Kleefisch-Jobst
Robert Konieczny
Igor Kovacevic
Leon Krier
Ivan Kucina
Christian Kühn
Alexandre Labasse
Juan José Lahuerta
Quim Larrea
Tomas Lauri
Kirsi Leiman
Janis Lejnieks
Mari Lending
Andres Lepik
Richard Levene
Blanca Lleó
Bart Lootsma
Jacques Lucan
Stuart MacDonald
Vittorio Magnago Lampugnani
Josep Lluís Mateo
Doriana O. Mandrelli
Fernando Márquez
Kent Martinussen
Marius Marcu-Lapadat
Roy Mänttäri

Fiona Meadows
Han Meyer
Eric Messerschmidt
Manuel Mendes
Ákos Moravánszky
Caroline Mierop
Frédéric Migayrou
Maciej Milobedzki
Vedran Mimica
Luca Molinari
Josep Mª Montaner
Rowan Moore
Vincent Morales Garoffolo
Haruo Morishima
Mohsen Mostafavi
Javier Mozas
Jorma Mukala
Patricia Muñiz
Christine Murray
Lucy Musgrave
Maroje Mrduljaš
Yves Nacher
Winfried Nerdinger
Pierluigi Nicolin
Riitta Nikula
Marja-Riitta Norri
Jürgen Nue Müller
Bitte Nygren
Werner Oechslin
Triin Ojari
Osamu Okamura
Nils-Ole Lund
Arjen Oosterman
John O'Regan
Shane O'Toole
Suha Özkan
Vlatko P. Korobar
Martin Paško
Béla Pazár
Wolfgang Pehnt
Víctor Pérez Escolano
Petros Phokaides
Ramón Pico Valimaña
Giacomo Polin
Yannos Politis
Ewa Porębska
Christophe Pourtois
Mercedes Planelles Herrero
Luigi Prestinenza
Jane Priestman
Michelle Provoost
György Radványi
Francis Rambert
Sixten Rahlff
Tatjana Rajic
Didier Rebois

Elias Redstone
Sebastian Redecke
Kristien Ring
Arno Ritter
Marina Romero
Aristides Romanos
Ilka & Andreas Ruby
Peter Rumpf
Roman Rutkowski
Raymund Ryan
Juan Antonio Sánchez Muñoz
Giampiero Sanguigni
Amber Sayah
Carole Schmit
Christian Schittich
Zenon Sierepeklis
Jasmina Siljanoska
Yorgos Simeoforidis
Marcel Smets
Georgi Stanishev
Lucien Steil
Dietmar Steiner
Lina Stergiou
Grzegorz Stiasny
Adolph Stiller
Socratis Stratis
Deyan Sudjic
Anca Sandu Tomasevschi
Maria Topolcanska
Ana Cristina Tostões
John Tuomey
Timo Tuomi
Elsa Turkusic
Huib van der Werf
Hans van Dijk
Roemer van Toorn
Katrien Vandermarliere
Jaume Valor
François Valentiny
Francy Valentiny
Yvette Vašourková
Joâo Vieira Caldas
Kjeld Vindum
Linda Vlassenrood
Vesna Vučinić
Wilfried Wang
Karin Winter
Ellis Woodman
Ana Maria Zahariade
Mirko Zardini
Elia Zenghelis
Artis Zvirgzdiņš

AAA, Shoqata e Arkitekteve të
Shqipërisë, Albania

BAIK, Bundeskammer der Architekten
und Ingenieurkonsulenten, Austria

FAB, Koninklijke Federatie van de
Architectenverenigingen van Belgïe,
Belgium

CNOA, Conseil National de l'Ordre des
Architectes, Belgium

Asocijacija Arhitekata u Bosni u
Hercegovini, Bosnia and Herzegovina

САБ, Съюз на архитектите в
България, Bulgaria

КАБ, Камарата на архитектите в
България, Bulgaria

UHA, Udruženje Hrvatskih Arhitekata,
Croatia

Σύλλογος Αρχιτεκτόνων Κύπρου,
Cyprus

ČKA, Česká komora architektů,
Czech Republic

AA Akademisk Arkitektforening,
Denmark

Danske Arkitektvirksomheder,
Denmark

EAL, Eesti Arhitektide Liit, Estonia

SAFA, Suomen Arkkitehtiliitto Finlands
Arkitektförbund, Finland

UNSFA, Union Nationale des Syndicats
Français d'Architectes, France

CIAF, Conseil International des
Architectes Français, France

Syndicat de l'Architecture, France

CNOA, Conseil National de l'Ordre des
Architectes, France

AAM, Асоцијација на архитекти
на Македонија, Former Yugoslav
Republic of Macedonia

VFA, Vereinigung Freischaffender
Architekten Deutschlands, Germany

BdB, Bund Deutscher Baumeister,
Architekten und Ingenieure, Germany

BDA, Bund Deutscher Architekten,
Germany

BAK, Bundesarchitektenkammer,
Germany

TEE, Τεχνικό Επιμελητήριο Ελλάδας,
Greece

Σ.Α.Δ.Α.Σ. - Π.Ε.Α.,
Συλλογοσ Αρχιτεκτονων
Διπλωματουχων Ανωτατων Σχολων
Πανελληνια Ενωση Αρχιτεκτονων,
Greece

MÉK, Magyar Építész Kamara, Hungary

RIAI, Royal Institute of the Architects of
Ireland, Ireland

CNAPPC, Consiglio Nazionale Degli
Architetti, Planificatori, Paesaggisti e
Conservatori

LAS, Latvijas Arhitektu savienības,
Latvia

LAS, Lietuvos architektų sąjunga,
Lithuania

OAI, Ordre des Architectes et des
Ingénieurs-Conseils, Luxembourg

KTP, Kamra tal-Periti, Malta

Arkitektbedriftene i Norge, Norway

NAL, Norske arkitekters landsforbunds,
Norway

IARP, Izba Architektów, Poland

Rzeczypospolitej Polskiej, Poland

Stowarzyszenie Architektów Polskich,
Poland

Ordem dos Arquitectos, Portugal

OAR, Ordinul Arhitecților din Romania,
Romania

SKA, Slovenská komora architektov,
Slovakia

ZAPS, Zbornica za arhitekturo in
prostor Slovenije, Slovenia

CSCAE, Consejo Superior de los
Colegios de Arquitectos de España,
Spain

SAR, Svenska Arkitekters Riksförbund,
Sweden

BNA, Bond van Nederlandse
Architecten, The Netherlands

Bureau Architectenregister,
The Netherlands

TMMOB Mimarlar Odası, Turkey

ARB, Architect's Registration Board,
United Kingdom

RIBA, Royal Institute of British
Architects, United Kingdom

Arkitektafélag Íslands, Iceland

Liechtensteinische Ingenieur-und
Architektenvereinigung, Liechtenstein

Union of Serbian Architects, Serbia

Association of Architects of
Montenegro

The Book

Published by
Actar Publishers
www.actar-d.com

Edited by
Fundació Mies van der Rohe
Diane Gray, Editor

Editorial Assistance
Mertitxell Cuspinera
Anna Bes
Núria Benages

Graphic Design
Papersdoc Design
Àngels Soler (Timeline)

Translation
Richard Lewis Rees

Photographs
Luis Asín, Iwan Baan, Dida Biggi, Hélène Binet, Eugeni Bofill/FRIS, Bitter Bredt, Federico Brunetti , Richard Bryant/Arcaid, Raimon Camprubi, David Cardelús, Lluís Casals, Paolo Catrica, Peter Cook, Richard Davies, Serge Demailly, Michel Denance , Marc de Blieck, Miguel de Guzmán, Luis Díaz Díaz, Filip Dujardin, Gilbert Fastenaekens, Guy Fehn, Georges Fessy, David Franck, Fernando Guerra/FG+SG, Philippe Guignard, Roland Halbe, Rob't Hart, Jiri Havran, Heinrich Helfenstein, José Hevia, Werner Hutmacher, Miran Kambič, Christian Kandzia, Klaus Kinold, Luuk Kramer, Martínez Lapeña – Torres, Robert Leš, Nic Lehoux, Jens Lindhe, Moreno Maggi, Duccio Malagamba, Daniel Malhão, Peter Mauss/Esto, Jürgen Mayer H., Phil Meech, Jean-Marie Monthiers, Rui Morais de Sousa, Stefan Müller-Naumann, Jeroen Musch, Daniel Osso, Jens Passoth, Joe Reid & John Peck, Christian Richters, Paolo Rosselli, Philippe Ruault, Pep Sau, Henry Pierre Schultz, Hisao Suzuki, Jörg von Bruchhausen, Deidi von Schaewen, Richard Walch, Hans Werlemann, Nigel Young, Ute Zscharnt, Gerald Zugmann, Kim Zwarts

Printing
Grafos. S.A.

Distribution
Actar D Inc. NY
151 Grand Street, 5th Floor
New York, NY 10013 USA
T + 41 61 5689 800
F + 41 61 5689 899

ISBN: 978-84-936901-6-8
Dip. Legal: B.14889-2013
The publication material for the projects has been provided by the architects

Printed and bound in the European Union.

 Culture

mies☐☐☐■ **barcelona**

 Generalitat de Catalunya
**Departament de Territori
i Sostenibilitat**

 GOBIERNO
DE ESPAÑA | MINISTERIO
DE FOMENTO

SPONSORED BY:

Fundació
BancSabadell

Roca

USM
Modular Furniture